ROCK BASS

2nd EDITION

By Jon Liebman
Foreword by Billy Sheehan

D0907693

RECORDING CREDITS
Bass: Jon Liebman
Drum programming: Jon Liebman
Guitar: Jake Reichbart
Engineering: Marty Liebman

ISBN 978-1-4803-5426-5

HAL•LEONARD®
CORPORATION

7777 W. BLUEMOUND RD. P.O. BOX 13819 MILWAUKEE, WI 53213

Visit Hal Leonard Online at
www.halleonard.com

ROCK BASS

CONTENTS

FOREWORD
BY BILLY SHEEHAN

Jon Liebman's wonderful book and accompanying CD, *Rock Bass*, is an essential tool for any bassist looking to expand their horizons as a player or to reinforce all that they may already know into a more solid foundation. Jon takes us through the decades of rock and popular bass playing, outlining and explaining every new development achieved by the greatest bass players throughout the history of rock 'n' roll.

The adventure of learning bass, or any instrument, never ends. Learning more about it can be accomplished in many ways, including listening, performing, writing, studying and more. Sitting down and working your way through this book will most certainly bring new ideas and approaches to any bassist who takes the time. And it will be time well spent. Bass on!

- Billy Sheehan

Billy Sheehan is a true bass legend, well known for his playing with Talas, Steve Vai, David Lee Roth, Mr. Big, Niacin and the Winery Dogs. Billy has earned numerous awards and distinctions for his bass playing, including multiple readers' polls from Guitar Player magazine, which also inducted him into its "Gallery of Greats." With his signature chording, two-handed tapping, right hand "three-finger picking" technique and controlled feedback, Billy Sheehan is said to be responsible for changing the way the bass is played today.

INTRODUCTION

There has never been anything else quite like rock 'n' roll—nor will there be. To call it "popular" would be to grossly understate its influence. To comment merely on the effect that it's had on society wouldn't do it justice either. Rock culture has permeated *virtually every facet of our lives.* It's impacted the way we dress, the way we speak, the way we walk. It's influenced our values, our social consciousness, and the way we raise our children. In the course of rock's history, we've seen a society that once extolled the virtues of wine, women, and song give way to a subculture that clamors for sex, drugs, and rock 'n' roll.

In *Rock Bass,* we'll approach the music from an historical perspective. We'll outline the events that were occurring behind the scenes so that they may serve as a backdrop to the music. I believe it's important to understand what was happening in American culture throughout each period—as well as the overall social conditions in the rest of the world. Historical milestones like the civil rights movement, the war in Vietnam, the unchecked entrepreneurial spirit, and the need for "alternative" methods of expression all had enormous impact on the music and culture of their day.

The core of this book is divided into six main chapters. The first five cover the history of rock bass from the fifties through the nineties. We'll begin with the types of grooves made famous by the likes of Chuck Berry and Buddy Holly and progress through the years, one decade at a time, to the hard rock sounds of the Red Hot Chili Peppers and the pop sounds of Hootie & the Blowfish. In between, we'll cover everyone from the Beatles to Deep Purple, the Pretenders to Pearl Jam. Each chapter will serve as an "encyclopedia" of grooves, capturing the essence of a particular decade of the rock 'n' roll era, including form, style, and historical significance—all from the standpoint of *(who else?!)* the rock bass player.

The last main chapter is devoted to building your rock vocabulary. It contains a series of "licks" that are common in rock music. These selections are not inherent to any particular decade of rock 'n' roll; rather, they are intended to showcase a wide variety of musical passages so you can familiarize yourself with the soloing aspect of rock 'n' roll. Diligent practice of these examples will round out your study of rock music in general, and rock bass in particular.

If you're familiar with my other Hal Leonard books and my websites, then you know my mantra (all together now...) *"Groove is everything, and everything must groove!"* It doesn't matter if you're playing rock 'n' roll, R&B, thrash, trash, funk, punk, bebop, hip-hop, classical, or Lawrence Welk; if you're not grooving, you're not playing the bass. Always work with a drum machine or, better yet, a real live drummer who can groove. At the very least, use a metronome. Always remember that your job is to groove with a great time feel.

Those of you who are familiar with my writing also know I'm a big advocate of being able to read and play in all keys. As I've stated before, there are no such things as "easy" keys and "hard" keys—only "familiar" keys and "unfamiliar" keys. We'll continue this approach in *Rock Bass*. (There's no reason you shouldn't be able to read and play "In-A-Gadda-Da-Vida" in, say, A♭ minor, for example.)

The appendix of this book offers an abundance of information about equipment and effects. Revised from the first edition of *Rock Bass*, it includes information on basses, strings, speakers, and amplification. What's more, it contains an overview of many different types of effects that you may want to use to enhance your sound. When I was a young student of bass, I wished I had one source that described, "What's a chorus?," "What's a flanger?," "What's digital delay?," etc. Now I have it. (The trouble is, I had to write it myself!) I think you'll find it useful.

As in my other books, I have also provided you with an extensive discography for recommended listening. In *Rock Bass,* however, the selections are organized not by bassist, but by decade. You'll find this approach much more practical than merely perusing a long list of bass players. (Actually, I wanted to save you the trouble of sifting through the Dave Clark Five and the Electric Prunes when you're really looking for Nine Inch Nails and Smashing Pumpkins!) Wherever possible, I've included the names of the primary bassist(s) for each group or artist. What's more, in this revised edition of *Rock Bass*, I've included a section in the discography called "The 2000s and beyond…" Here I've listed newer releases from several die-hard rockers, like Black Sabbath, Metallica and Rush, as well as many new names that were not included (or in some cases, even around) when *Rock Bass* was first published. They include everyone from Avenged Sevenfold and Breaking Benjamin to Fall Out Boy, Five Finger Death Punch, Halestorm, Nickelback, Slipknot, Stone Sour and many others.

Though you'll have to work hard in playing your way through this book, I *am* going to lift one of my customary restrictions. (Hey, it's only rock 'n' roll…) If you're like me, you like to go through everything from left to right, from top to bottom, one page at a time, in the precise order in which it's presented; this particular type of discipline, however, is *not* crucial in the study of *Rock Bass*. Progressing through this book in order *will* provide you with a good sense of the evolution of rock bass from the beginning—and I strongly suggest you spend some time on each chapter so you become proficient in all the styles presented here—but I leave the order up to your own discretion. So if you've got a hankering for a driving, steady eighth-note Van-Halen thing one day and a bouncy McCartney-style thing the next day, go for it.

The CD that accompanies *Rock Bass* includes every musical selection in this book, with drums and guitar (complete with distortion, overdrive, and all that other stuff rock guitarists love to use!). As in my other books, the bass is panned all the way to the right, so you can turn it down and play along with the rhythm section. You also have the option of isolating the bass so you can hear the nuances in my playing.

By the time you complete this book, you'll have a panoramic view of the history of rock 'n' roll. You'll be able to follow the history of American culture, as well as the impact of the "British Invasion" throughout the last half of the twentieth century. You'll be familiar with all the major styles of rock bass, from the beginning. You'll have a basic understanding of the wide variety of equipment and effects used in today's musical environments. You'll also have a list of recordings telling you where to find some of the most historically significant music ever produced.

You'll need to work hard and practice properly. You'll need to take it seriously. (Yes, rock 'n' roll *is* serious business.) Your primary goal should be to have the ability to make up your own bass lines in any particular rock style, rather than to learn and memorize a bunch of "exercises." The point is that the selections contained herein are not intended to be practiced as a series of exercises, but rather as *music*. Never lose sight of the music.

Peace, love, and rock 'n' roll!

J.L.

'50s

The '50s

POLITICS AND CULTURE

In the 1950s, countries were still trying to "get back to normal" following World War II. However, the turbulence was far from over. The United States was soon at war again, this time in Korea. Senator Joseph McCarthy embarked on a twentieth-century "witch hunt" for communists across the U.S. In Montgomery, Alabama, Rosa Parks caused what was to become a seminal incident in the civil rights movement when she refused to give up her bus seat to a white passenger. At the end of the decade, Fidel Castro was staging a revolution in Cuba.

Several notable events, on the happier side, also occurred during the fifties. Diner's Club introduced the first credit card. Disneyland opened in California. Ray Kroc founded the McDonald's Corporation. The U.S. government approved Jonas Salk's vaccine for polio. Congress passed the Interstate Highway Act. The U.S.S.R. launched Sputnik, the first artificial earth satellite, into orbit, inaugurating the space age.

As is usually the case, the younger generation developed new forms of expression and style. Bobby socks and poodle skirts became fashionable, as did coonskin caps and cigarette packs rolled up in T-shirt sleeves. The movies of the day were *Blackboard Jungle, Guys & Dolls,* and *Rebel Without a Cause.* On TV, Americans were watching "I Love Lucy," "Father Knows Best," and "Leave It to Beaver."

MUSIC

The music of the day responded in kind to the social circumstances. The post-war climate called for different sounds and a new feeling beyond the big band and swing styles of Benny Goodman and Glenn Miller. As the music world entered the 1950s, Charlie Parker and Dizzy Gillespie were developing their new bebop sound, where the concept of a singer fronting a band was replaced by small instrumental groups playing fast, often unsingable melodies with extremely complex harmonies. At the same time, Dave Brubeck, Gerry Mulligan, Miles Davis, Lennie Tristano, and several others were formulating the "cool school" of west coast jazz.

Amidst all this activity, the public was losing its ability to identify with much of the music of the times. People found themselves unable to sing along with these new sounds which, for the most part, they didn't understand.

During this period, a new style called "rhythm and blues" (R&B) developed as a follow-up to the big band era of the thirties and forties. This music is considered one of the earliest forms of rock 'n' roll. R&B was characterized by smaller groups (trios, quartets, quintets), syncopated rhythms, and a heavier backbeat on the drums. The development of the electric guitar played an important role in this new style, thanks to Les Paul (yes, there actually was a *person* named Les Paul), who popularized the instrument. The saxophone was prominent in this new sound, as well.

Rock 'n' roll started to emerge around 1955 when Bill Haley & the Comets came on the scene, along with Elvis Presley, who had begun recording in 1954. By the time Elvis appeared on the Ed Sullivan Show in 1956, he was already a teen idol. The term "rock 'n' roll" was coined by Alan Freed, a disk jockey in Cleveland, upon observing a surge in the popularity of this new style of music.

Interestingly, what was eventually to become one of the most important elements in the evolution of rock 'n' roll was the development of the electric bass. (Once again, we saved the day!) Leo Fender, considered the father of the electric bass, had been experimenting with instruments and amplifiers in his radio shop during World War II. His first electric bass guitar, the Fender Precision Bass, was created in 1951.

Most of the earliest rock bands, however, still utilized the upright bass rather than the electric. Not only was the electric bass brand new, but it was initially met with a great deal of opposition and resistance. People didn't understand it. They didn't take it seriously. It wasn't until its potential as a rhythm instrument became known—along with its ability to enhance the feeling of the music with its "new sound"—that the electric bass became appreciated and widely used. And the rest, as they say, is history.

In addition to Elvis Presley and Bill Haley & the Comets, some of the earliest rock groups and artists included Chuck Berry, Little Richard, Bobby Darin, Eddie Cochran, Bo Diddley, Ritchie Valens, Carl Perkins, Gene Vincent, Fats Domino, Jerry Lee Lewis, the Big Bopper, the Everly Brothers, Buddy Holly & the Crickets, Danny & the Juniors, the Crew Cuts, the Diamonds, the Platters, the Coasters, and others.

The discography in the back of this book lists many artists and select recordings that provide a valuable resource for studying the roots of rock 'n' roll. Be sure to do some listening in order to understand the essence of the music. You might want to tune in some of the oldies stations on the radio to familiarize yourself with these styles. Maybe your mom or dad might have some recordings in their record collection (or maybe your grandma and grandpa, for that matter!). Of course, nowadays, there's virtually no limit to what you can find on iTunes, YouTube and many other sources, so you really have no excuse!

THE GROOVES

Swing/Shuffle. Many of the earliest rock grooves from the fifties, right on the heels of the jazz/ big band era, were based on blues or blues-oriented patterns and had a swing/shuffle feel. These selections sound good on the upright bass and you may want to give them a try if you're an upright player. (In fact, on the accompanying CD, grooves 1.3 and 1.4 are played on the upright bass for the sake of authenticity—and, well… for fun!) If you're not an upright player, don't worry. They sound just fine on electric bass, too.

The 12/8 Feel. One of the most characteristic sounds of fifties rock makes use of the 12/8 feel. There are countless songs from this period in 12/8 using a I–vi–IV–V or a I–vi–ii–V pattern. Though these grooves are written in 12/8, the backbeat on "two" and "four" (or, technically, "four" and "ten") became an important part of the overall sound and feel, as you'll hear on the drum patterns on the CD. Practice grooves 1.6 through 1.8. If you've ever listened to any fifties music, this should be a very familiar sound to you.

Straight Eighths. As the decade progressed, much of the music started moving away from the triplet subdivision (one-two-three-*four*-five six, seven-eight-nine-*ten*-eleven-twelve) to a heavier, more rock-oriented straight-eighth-note subdivision (one-and-*two-and*-three-and-*four*-and, one-and-*two-and*-three-and-*four*-and). This pattern became quite popular in the sixties, as you'll see in Chapter 2, though its origin is actually in the fifties. Grooves 1.9 through 1.12 offer a hint of what lies ahead.

The "Bounce" Feel. Another extremely popular rock bass pattern from the fifties was a sort of "bounce" feel, which helped create a new type of drive and energy. The I–vi–IV–V and I–vi–ii–V progressions were quite common in this style. Grooves using this pattern were often developed by arpeggiating the chord changes. The straight-eighth subdivision was common, although the triplet or swing feel was used as well.

"Whole Lotta Shakin' Goin' On..."

The fifties had proven to be a most important period in the development of rock 'n' roll (and rock bass). A solid foundation had been laid, and an entirely new sound was introduced. Though the world was not without its share of problems, people seemed to be in a different, much happier state of mind—especially when compared to that of the previous decade. New messages were being transmitted. A new generation was coming of age. And yet, it was only the beginning. No one could have ever guessed what was to follow.

'60s

The '60s

POLITICS AND CULTURE

The 1960s ushered in a new era with new methods of self-expression. As the baby boom was winding down, people were discovering different ways of looking at the world. New types of thinking were introduced, giving way to the formation of new movements and organizations. Society continued to move forward, testing the limits of what was considered proper and acceptable. There were "revolutionary" hair styles, clothes, and, of course, music. At the same time, advances were made in the fields of art, medicine, and technology. The sixties brought about a metamorphosis of thought and philosophy, which yielded many milestones of great historical significance. It was a controversial decade, to say the least.

In 1960, the birth control pill was introduced and quickly became a catalyst in what would come to be known as the "sexual revolution." In 1962, Rachel Carson published *Silent Spring,* launching a new environmental awareness across the U.S. and beyond. An early-sixties Andy Warhol exhibit featured a Campbell's Soup can in a New York gallery, giving birth to the "pop art" movement. The U.S. Surgeon General issued the first warnings of the hazards of cigarette smoking.

Congress passed the Civil Rights Act. Ralph Nader published *Unsafe at Any Speed,* initiating a movement on behalf of consumer rights. The National Organization for Women (N.O.W.) was formed, launching a new era of feminism and women's rights. Dr. Christiaan Barnard made medical history by performing the first human heart transplant. The U.S. Department of Defense launched the Advanced Research Project Agency Network (ARPANET) which eventually became the Internet. Neil Armstrong became the first human ever to set foot on the moon.

But the decade of the 1960s did not go without its share of unrest and turbulence. Civil disturbances, assassinations, and upheavals were becoming increasingly common. In the U.S., it seemed that trouble was brewing everywhere. Racial tensions were becoming rampant. Riots broke out in the part of Los Angeles known as Watts in 1965, furthering the black-white dissension that already existed. Malcolm X was assassinated that same year. The Black Panther party was formed in Oakland, California in 1966. Civil rights leader Martin Luther King, Jr. was slain in 1968.

Politics were by no means exempt from the discord. President Kennedy was assassinated in 1963. His brother, Bobby, a presidential hopeful himself, was murdered in 1968. Even the music world had its share of tragedy during this period, including the violence and death that occurred during a Rolling Stones performance at the Altamont Free Festival in California, where the Hell's Angels were hired to provide the security.

And trouble was not limited to the U.S. The Cuban Missile Crisis was unfolding in 1962. The Cold War with the Soviet Union was ever present. The war in Vietnam was increasing in magnitude. Israel fought the Six Day War against Egypt and its Arab allies, under the direction of Moshe Dayan in 1967.

The generation gap was becoming more and more pronounced. Young people spoke out and rebelled against the wealth and success of their parents' generation. Those not in favor of dramatic change responded with pet phrases such as "America: love it or leave it," adding to the already present tensions.

A hippie movement began to form. Protests were held in the name of peace, with messages of "stop the war" along with "flower power" and love-ins. The drug culture was ever present. Marijuana and LSD grew enormously popular with the younger generation. The late Timothy Leary was advising young people to "turn on, tune in, drop out."

MUSIC

Art and music were being stretched to the most extreme forms of experimentation, incorporating elements of colors, psychedelic images, electronics, and spaciness. The common underlying sentiment was that of change and rebellion. The Who sang "I hope I die before I get old" in "My Generation." Ten Years After had a big hit with "I'd Love to Change the World." The Beatles were singing "Revolution." These are but a few examples of how the music of the day was affected by the social climate.

Though turbulence existed throughout most of the decade, not everything about the sixties was seeded in anger and protest. The sixties also gave us "The Dick Van Dyke Show," hoola-hoops, Apollo rockets, and Joe Namath.

Many of the bands of the decade were less controversial, even innocent, particularly toward the early years. Chubby Checker was doing "The Twist," the Beach Boys built a loyal following singing about California surf music, and Tommy James & the Shondells sang "My baby does the Hanky Panky" (though "Crimson and Clover," toward the end of the decade, had a whole different vibe!). Other popular acts from this time included Dion & the Belmonts, Jan & Dean, and Roy Orbison.

Rock 'n' roll, no longer a novelty, began to branch out in several directions simultaneously. Dozens of new styles were developed, each distinct in its own way and enormously influential to the evolution of twentieth-century music. The music was no longer simply "rock 'n' roll." New forms of rock were being discovered all over the place.

One of the most influential and highly successful producers (not just from the sixties, but throughout rock history) was Phil Spector. Spector became a pioneer in the production of rock records with his famous "wall of sound." Rather than limiting his focus and concentration to just the music (though his accolades in this regard are most noteworthy), he would experiment with varying sizes of groups and instrumentation, as well as new techniques with reverb and echo. Spector had enormous success with groups like the Crystals, the Ronettes, the Shirelles, the Teddy Bears, the Chiffons, the Righteous Brothers, Ike & Tina Turner, and others.

Meanwhile…

A folk/rock movement began to take root, injecting elements of rock into music that was inspired by folk acts such as Peter, Paul & Mary and Pete Seeger. Among the most influential folk/rock artists were Bob Dylan, the Lovin' Spoonful, Simon & Garfunkel, the Byrds, and Scottish singer Donovan.

Meanwhile…

Berry Gordy was having tremendous success in Detroit with his Motown label. The music, recorded mostly by black artists, reflected a grittier, more urban, soulful sound, integrating the earthiest elements of R&B. Among the most popular Motown artists were the Marvelettes, the Supremes, the Four Tops, the Temptations, Marvin Gaye, Stevie Wonder, Junior Walker, Jackie Wilson, Mary Wells, Martha Reeves & the Vandellas, Smokey Robinson & the Miracles, and many others. The session players that made it happen for virtually all the Motown hits were known collectively as the Funk Brothers. The Brothers included keyboardist Earl Van Dyke, guitarists Joe Messina and Robert White, saxophonists Hank Cosby and Mike Terry, and several other notable musicians who rounded out the group. Perhaps the most prominent and influential Funk Brothers were drummer Benny Benjamin and bassist James Jamerson.

At the same time, a similar style was being developed in the deep south. A new breed of "southern soul" was taking root in places like Memphis, Tennessee and Muscle Shoals, Alabama. The Stax (Stax/Volt) Record label was, perhaps, the most prominent in this genre. Among the more notable acts were Wilson Pickett, Curtis Mayfield, Sam & Dave, Percy Sledge, Otis Redding, Aretha Franklin, and others. The driving force behind this music was a group known as Booker T. & the MGs, featuring organist Booker T. Jones, along with guitarist Steve Cropper, bassist Donald "Duck" Dunn, and drummer Al Jackson, Jr. This style became prevalent in other parts of the U.S., as well, including Chicago, New York, and other cities. The soulful music of Ray Charles and James Brown was becoming increasingly popular, too.

Meanwhile …

Rock 'n' roll had become the rage, not just in America but in Europe as well, particularly in England. The phenomenon known as "the British Invasion" began to take place around 1964 when the Beatles took the world by storm. The songwriting duo of John Lennon and Paul McCartney, compounded with the brilliant work of producer George Martin, the presentation and overall "look" influenced by manager Brian Epstein, and the general charisma of John, Paul, George, and Ringo, just "hit the spot," catching the world completely off guard. Around the same time, the Rolling Stones were acquiring a great deal of notoriety, as well. Where the Beatles' music was characterized by singable melodies and tight harmonies, the Stones' music was centered more around rhythmic variations and guitar riffs, supplied by Keith Richards. The Dave Clark Five, the Searchers, Peter & Gordon, the Animals, and Chad & Jeremy were all part of the initial British Invasion, too.

Other British groups to follow included the Kinks, the Yardbirds, Freddie & the Dreamers, Herman's Hermits, Cream (featuring Eric Clapton, Jack Bruce, and Ginger Baker), Manfred Mann, Ten Years After, the Hollies, the Moody Blues, the Spencer Davis Group, The Who, the Troggs, T-Rex, Rod Stewart, and many others.

Meanwhile…

An "underground" movement of rock 'n' roll started to develop, most notably on the U.S. west coast in the Haight-Ashbury district of San Francisco. (Promoter Bill Graham described underground music as "just any band that ain't had a hit yet.") Included among the bands that emerged from Haight-Ashbury were Jefferson Airplane, the Grateful Dead, the Electric Prunes, the Strawberry Alarm Clock, Moby Grape, and the Quicksilver Messenger Service. Other notable San Francisco bands were Big Brother & the Holding Company (featuring Janis Joplin) and Santana.

New York also had its own underground movement taking shape. The Velvet Underground, featuring Lou Reed and Nico, was formed under the mentorship, to some extent, of artist Andy Warhol. England had yet another form of underground rock 'n' roll which included Pink Floyd and Social Deviants.

Meanwhile…

Throughout the decade, a melting pot ensued with all sorts of groups sprouting up all over the place, each with a different sound and a variety of messages. Among the more "middle of the road" type groups were the Four Seasons, the Mamas & the Papas, the Monkees, the Rascals, and the Turtles. Creedence Clearwater Revival was tremendously popular, with hits like "Proud Mary," "Green River," "Suzie-Q," and many others. Jimi Hendrix came on the scene in 1966 with "Hey, Joe" and began having incalculable influence on guitar players, leaving a legacy that will endure for untold years. Other prominent rock groups of the sixties included Sly & the Family Stone, Steppenwolf, the Amboy Dukes (featuring Ted Nugent, the Motor City Madman!), the Doors, Vanilla Fudge, and lots of others.

Let's get to the bass, already!

Before the sixties, it was not common to find many musicians who were well known specifically for playing the bass. Naturally, a few exceptions existed in classical music (Domenico Dragonetti, Giovanni Botessini) and jazz (Jimmy Blanton, Scott La Faro). During the sixties, the first generation of rock and R&B bass heroes began to emerge. Among the pioneers were Larry Graham, Jack Bruce, Jerry Jemmott, Noel Redding, Donald "Duck" Dunn, Jack Casady, John Entwistle, Paul McCartney, Carol Kaye, Tim Bogert, and the immortal James Jamerson, to name but a few. In subsequent decades, the number of influential rock bass players grew to a staggering number (as you'll soon discover).

As rock music made the transition from the fifties into the sixties, it was still not unheard of for some of the earliest sixties rock bands to use an upright bass. By the end of the decade, though, use of the upright was virtually nonexistent in rock 'n' roll. You can try some of these grooves on an upright if you want to (if you have one, and if you can!). Generally speaking, though, your electric will be more authentic.

Among the most common characteristics of this music is the influence of the blues (always a prevalent pattern in pop music, rock, jazz and…well… *the blues!*). A driving backbeat is nearly always present, whether the music is fast or slow. Much of sixties rock was influenced by the psychedelic craze, use of electronics, and sometimes just general weirdness. Make sure you use the discography to hear as much of this music as possible; otherwise, it loses much of its meaning.

THE GROOVES

As you can see, we have a lot to keep in mind when playing rock bass from the sixties. Following is a cross-section of different types of bass grooves in the styles of 1960s rock 'n' roll. As we've been saying, the types of music throughout this period are quite diverse. Therefore, I've attempted to give you a little bit of everything here. Don't forget your metronome, drum machine, or drummer (ever!). Again, all of the grooves in this book are included on the CD. Listen closely, concentrate, and groove! All set? Let's trip through the sixties.

Straight Eighths. One of the main elements distinguishing sixties rock from the earliest styles is
the use of the eighth-note subdivision, as opposed to the triplet, or shuffle, subdivision. The pulse was
provided by a straight eighth-note feel, with a backbeat. Blues and blues-based patterns were still very
common.

Syncopation. As the eighth-note rock style continued to develop in the sixties, varying degrees of syncopation (strong accents on "weak" beats) were introduced.

Triplet Subdivision. Though the straight-eighth-note feel was prominent, the triplet subdivision was not altogether gone. The following grooves are reminiscent of the sixties' spy movies. The feel includes elements of blues and soul, too. Notice the interpretation while listening to the CD.

The "Motown" Sound. The Motown sound was a form of R&B, urban by nature. The music created a driving force, with elements of funk and blues and a heavy backbeat.

"Turn, Turn, Turn..."

By the end of the sixties, rock 'n' roll was stronger than ever, with loads of different "scenes" in full force throughout the U.S and Europe. Led Zeppelin and Jethro Tull both released their debut albums in 1969. Several rock festivals were organized, including the Monterey Pop Festival, Newport Rock '69, and the tragic Altamont Free Festival. England had its share of festivals too, including the Isle of Wight Festival, featuring Bob Dylan, The Who, and the Moody Blues. Around the same time, in 1969, about 400,000 rock 'n' roll lovers gathered at old Max Yasgur's farm in upstate New York for the Woodstock festival, perhaps the best known of all the festivals. Among the many performers were Joe Cocker, Santana, Arlo Guthrie, Richie Havens, Country Joe & the Fish, Ten Years After, Jefferson Airplane, John Sebastian, and Crosby, Stills & Nash. The new culture was alive and well and showed no signs of slowing down.

'70s

The '70s

POLITICS AND CULTURE

By the end of the 1960s, the hippie generation had made its point—the population had spoken out on sex, civil rights, and the war in Vietnam. At the dawn of the new decade, young people continued to find plenty of things to protest, yet at the same time, they discovered new diversions and new forms of self-expression. Though the 1970s contended with many of the same issues as the previous ten years, the new decade developed an identity all its own.

Americans were asked to conserve gasoline and electricity while the world was in the throes of a panic-evoking energy crisis. In the controversial Roe vs. Wade case, the U.S. Supreme Court ruled that women have the right to an abortion. Muhammad Ali knocked out George Foreman and regained his title as heavyweight boxing champion of the world in the fight that would become known as the "Rumble in the Jungle." The personal computer was first introduced when the "Altair 8800" was advertised in Popular Electronics magazine as a $400 build-it-yourself kit for hobbyists. Richard Nixon became the only person ever to resign from the U.S presidency in the aftermath of the Watergate scandal. Lesley Brown gave birth to the first test-tube baby.

The decade had its share of unrest and disturbances, too. In the "Jonestown Massacre" in Guyana, over 900 people died after drinking cyanide-laced punch in a mass suicide led by the Reverend Jim Jones. The Ayatollah Khomeini became the ruler of Iran after leading an Islamic revolution against the Shah. The existence of South Vietnam came to an end with the fall of Saigon in 1975 after a loss of approximately 750,000 lives and $140 billion. By the end of the seventies, Russia was invading Afghanistan in the name of a Marxist government.

Still, life went on and all facets of society continued to evolve and flourish. Moviegoers flocked to the theaters to see *Jaws* and *Star Wars*. One of the most significant events in the history of television occurred when some 130 million Americans found themselves entranced during the eight-night mini-series "Roots," based on a novel by Alex Haley. "Marcus Welby, M.D.," "All in the Family," "The Brady Bunch," "Charlie's Angels," and "Starsky & Hutch" were other popular shows that permeated the U.S. culture during the seventies.

There was a feeling of openness and a spirit of freedom in the seventies. Styles became more liberal, even outlandish. Customized vans, often with very elaborate paint jobs, were seen just about everywhere in the seventies. Platform shoes were the rage. Loud print shirts with open collars were popular. Leisure suits, sideburns, long hair (including oversized Afros), and short shorts called "hot pants" were all fads that swept the seventies.

MUSIC

In response to the social climate of the time, an interesting phenomenon occurred. By the seventies, the earliest rock fans were already in their thirties. For the first time, there were actually two generations of rock fans. The older group followed a range of artists from Elvis Presley and Little Richard to the Doors and the Animals, while the younger generation was more partial to some of the newer groups, like Led Zeppelin, Jethro Tull, and Crosby, Stills & Nash.

By the very early part of the decade, the Beatles and the Supremes had disbanded, and Jimi Hendrix and Janis Joplin were dead. Rock continued to branch out in many directions. The music sounded different now. Artists like Blondie, the Police, and the Boomtown Rats were making their way onto the scene. A punk movement began forming with groups like Iggy & the Stooges (featuring Iggy Pop), Adam & the Ants, the Clash, the Sex Pistols (with Sid Vicious and Johnny Rotten), Siouxsie & the Banshees, and others. Frank Zappa, a most unique innovator, was playing to packed houses throughout the U.S. and abroad. Groups like Roxy Music, the Pretenders, and Queen were becoming increasingly well known.

Mainstream rock 'n' roll during the seventies was made up of groups like Chicago, the Eagles, Fleetwood Mac, the Doobie Brothers, Foreigner, Boston, Genesis, Bachman-Turner Overdrive, and Grand Funk. Other popular artists/groups from this period included Jackson Browne, Paul Simon, Stevie Wonder, Seals & Crofts, Badfinger, the Guess Who, Blue Öyster Cult, the Hollies, and Poco. Still other acts that enjoyed success in the seventies were Jeff Beck, the J. Geils Band, Traffic, Mountain, Mott the Hoople, Yes, and Emerson, Lake & Palmer.

In an entirely different circle, the soul and urban movement continued to flourish. Artists such as George Clinton, Isaac Hayes, Rick James, Curtis Mayfield, James Brown, Prince, and Barry White were all quite popular. And groups such as Earth, Wind & Fire, the O'Jays, the Ohio Players, and Sly & the Family Stone were all going strong.

Some groups, like Lynryd Skynyrd and the Allman Brothers Band, injected elements of country music into their sound, formulating a "southern rock" movement. In other environments, "concept" bands, including Pink Floyd and the Electric Light Orchestra, were beginning to emerge.

During the seventies, a generation of bonafide rock idols was born and/or catapulted to superstardom. Included among this group were David Bowie, Bruce Springsteen, Eric Clapton, Alice Cooper, Bob Seger, Elton John, Billy Joel, Peter Frampton, and several others.

At the same time, a hard rock/early metal movement was getting underway. The artists and groups in this category are among the most popular in rock history. They include Aerosmith, Led Zeppelin, Black Sabbath, Deep Purple, Jethro Tull, King Crimson, Kiss, Rush, Van Halen, Ted Nugent, and many more.

By the seventies, bass players had still not received full-fledged "rock star" status. However, the next generation provided a new group of influential bassists who were making their way onto the scene. Among the young lions were Geezer Butler, Geddy Lee, Bootsy Collins, John Paul Jones, Chris Squire, Verdine White, Gene Simmons, Phil Chen, and others.

THE GROOVES

Much of the music of the seventies was characterized by dance-like rhythms, with a driving, straight-eighth-note feel. Octave patterns were enormously popular during this period. Sixteenth-note patterns, dotted rhythms, and funk-oriented grooves were common as well. Swing and shuffle feels were not as widely used as those with eighth-note subdivisions, though they still had their place in this music—these types of grooves are often "can't miss" crowd-pleasers, especially when performed live. Hard driving rock, now in its post-psychedelic stage, was quite well-developed by this point.

This chapter provides a cross-section of all of these styles. In order to get the feel for this music, try to picture yourself in the middle of the seventies scene. Think about what was going on in the world at the time. Practice these grooves carefully and accurately with your metronome, drum machine, or real live drummer. See if you can get a hold of some of the recordings listed in the discography. Most of this music is still readily available, especially on iTunes, YouTube, Pandora, Spotify, etc. You're now in the next phase of the time warp. Hang on, now. Here we go!

Dance Rhythms. Grooves 3.1 through 3.7 are dance-oriented rhythms with a strong backbeat and a driving pulse. Many of these examples contain the signature octave patterns that were so widely used in the seventies. Make sure you practice these patterns accurately and precisely.

Sixteenth-Note Variations. Some of the bass lines tended to get a bit more intricate during the seventies, making use of different variations of sixteenth-note patterns. Octaves were still part of the mix, as was the strong backbeat. Try these grooves.

Sixteenth-Note Variations. Some of the bass lines tended to get a bit more intricate during the seventies, making use of different variations of sixteenth-note patterns. Octaves were still part of the mix, as was the strong backbeat. Try these grooves.

Sixteenth-Note Variations. Some of the bass lines tended to get a bit more intricate during the seventies, making use of different variations of sixteenth-note patterns. Octaves were still part of the mix, as was the strong backbeat. Try these grooves.

Sixteenth-Note Variations. Some of the bass lines tended to get a bit more intricate during the seventies, making use of different variations of sixteenth-note patterns. Octaves were still part of the mix, as was the strong backbeat. Try these grooves.

Funk. Funk had become enormously popular in the seventies, standing on its own merits, as well as crossing over into R&B and jazz. Naturally, rock and pop music got a piece of the funk action, too. [*]

[*] Many more funk grooves can be found in my other Hal Leonard books, most notably *Funk Bass, Funk/Fusion Bass, Bass Grooves: The Ultimate Collection* and *Bass Aerobics*.

Triplet Subdivision. As we've discussed, use of the triplet subdivision was not the norm any more by this time, yet there's something about a blues or blues-style shuffle that makes people feel good. Rock 'n' roll is no exception!

Hard Rock. By the end of the seventies, hard rock had amassed a huge following. This music still contained elements widely used up to this point, namely, blues-based progressions and a heavy backbeat. Hard rock, though, had a stronger, more powerful sound. The electronics tended to make use of distortion and different types of delay, making the sound distinctly different from the spacy, psychedelic experiments from a decade earlier.

"Reelin' in the Years..."

As the seventies came to a close, friction and tensions in the world abounded once again. Double-digit inflation and skyrocketing unemployment rates plagued the U.S. economy. Iran had captured over fifty Americans and held them prisoner for over a year. Chrysler Corporation was on the brink of bankruptcy.

Meanwhile, a quarter of a century had passed since the dawn of rock 'n' roll. So many scenes had developed. So much had been going on simultaneously. What could possibly happen next? The world was ready for a change. It is unlikely, however, that it was prepared for what happened next.

'80s

The '80s

POLITICS AND CULTURE

The eighties would become a decade of great historical significance. The world experienced many changes that would have a profound impact on government, economy, culture (including art and music), and the population's general health and well-being.

In 1980, Ted Turner launched his Cable News Network (CNN), which was the first 24-hour, all-news TV station. Americans were also faithfully watching "The Cosby Show," "Dallas," "Cheers," and "Miami Vice." At the movies, people were paying to see *Fame, E.T., Top Gun, Fatal Attraction,* and *Dirty Dancing.*

Not everything that occurred during the eighties was of a joyous nature. In fact, many discoveries and events sent the world into near panic. The AIDS virus was identified early in the decade and was compared by researchers to the bubonic plague pandemic of the thirteenth century and other deadly diseases cited as far back as the old testament. Crack cocaine appeared on America's streets and rapidly gained popularity. A poison gas leak from a Union Carbide pesticide plant in Bhopal, India caused the worst industrial accident in history, killing thousands of people and injuring hundreds of thousands.

Globally, several critical developments were unfolding during the eighties. Iraq was invading Iran in an attempt to overthrow the Khomeini regime. Millions of people across the world spoke out in protest over Apartheid in South Africa. Soviet Premier Mikhail Gorbachev introduced the concepts of *glasnost* and *perestroika* (openness and restructuring), in hopes of increasing democracy, free enterprise, and improved relations with the West. Germany's Berlin Wall was taken down, thus reuniting communist East Berlin with democratic West Berlin. The European Single Act was signed, bringing down trade barriers throughout Europe, combining participating nations into a single unified market. Delegates from twenty-four countries around the world convened in Montreal, Canada and called for a ban on chlorofluorocarbons (CFCs) in an attempt to preserve the earth's ozone layer.

The eighties are often referred to as the decade of greed or the "me" generation. People turned inward. The emphasis was on the individual rather than the community. Products such as the Sony Walkman and the inundation of "self-this" and "self-that" products substantiate this point. The customized vans from the seventies gave way to Volvos and BMWs for those who could afford them. Instant gratification became an obsession. Overindulgence in cocaine, "ecstasy," and other drugs was the norm among the "in" crowds.

Under the guise of an entrepreneurial spirit, the eighties were fraught with mergers, acquisitions, junk bonds, and highly leveraged buyouts. "Reaganomics" became a widely used term, coined by journalists in reference to America's financial well-being. An awful lot of people got rich during this period, but it was only a matter of time until things caught up to them. By the end of the decade, President George H.W. Bush had to persuade Congress to vote in favor of giving $166 billion to save the U.S. savings and loan industry, setting off the largest federal bailout in history.

MUSIC

As far as music was concerned, at least two developments had a tremendous impact on the music industry during the eighties. One was the launching of the Music Television (MTV) Network, early in the decade. Suddenly, the way artists appeared became so enormously important, it was almost as if the music was secondary; it became crucial for rock artists not only to be concerned about their sound, but also the importance of "the look." MTV propelled the music industry with a whole new kind of momentum.

Another significant milestone of the eighties was the development and popularity of compact discs (CDs). The record industry had suffered setbacks and financial burdens until CDs became available. Fortunately for the record companies, CDs became tremendously popular almost immediately. People no longer had to worry about scratchy vinyl and the "kid glove" care required for maintaining record albums. CDs, we were told, would never wear out and would provide flawless, brilliant sound reproduction forever.*

It is interesting to note that not all of the sentiment during the eighties was that of selfishness and greed. Musicians joined forces numerous times throughout the decade, embarking on several full-scale projects intended to reach out and help those less fortunate. The "Feed the World" song, the "Do They Know It's Christmas?" recording and the "U.S.A. for Africa" project drew dozens of celebrities together, all donating their talents. Both records raised millions of dollars for their respective causes. The "Band Aid," "Live Aid," and "Farm Aid" concerts evoked a similar spirit of people helping people.

So where was rock 'n' roll in the midst of all this activity? As the genre continued to branch out, the eighties provided something for everyone, serving up a wide assortment of rock 'n' roll styles.

Many pop-oriented groups started going for a cleaner, purer, more precise kind of sound. Included among these bands were Tears for Fears, Culture Club, Depeche Mode, Wham!, Duran Duran, Spandau Ballet, the Eurhythmics, the Pretenders, the Police, the Pet Shop Boys, the Human League, and others. George Michael, Elvis Costello, and several other solo artists were also considered to be within this realm. For the most part, these groups tended to be less guitar-driven and placed more emphasis on synthesizers and drum machines, though exceptions did exist.

Folk-oriented rock still had a following in the eighties, as performed by Suzanne Vega, Tracy Chapman, and Billy Bragg. A blue collar type of rock 'n' roll went over very big also, through the hands of John Cougar Mellencamp and Bruce Springsteen. Michael Jackson became one of the biggest names in music during the eighties, as his compelling metamorphosis continued to develop, from the preteen lead singer of the Jackson 5 to the eccentric, controversial pop icon atop the music charts.

Rock 'n' roll was by no means for men only. Women had been providing important contributions to the rock scene almost from the beginning (e.g., the Supremes, Lesley Gore, Mary Wells, and many others). By the eighties, though, most of the female rock celebrities had shed their "nice girl" image— thanks, largely to Janis Joplin, Grace Slick, and a few other pioneers who had paved the way. Most of the female groups and pop stars during this time had grown more irreverent. Bands such as the Go-Gos, the Bangles, and Bananarama had each developed a huge following. Madonna and Cyndi Lauper had attained superstar status. Tina Turner and Janet Jackson were also luminaries during the eighties. Other popular female rock stars included Joan Jett, Pat Benatar, and Stevie Nicks.

Though hints of it can be found in earlier music, rap music gained widespread acceptance during the eighties. This music was based on very heavy backbeats (nearly always supplied by drum machines) and repetitive, deep, reverberating bass lines (nearly always supplied by synthesizers). The vocals were spoken, and in many cases shouted, to the rhythm of the music. For a while, it seemed as though nearly everyone was touting themselves as a rap singer. Quite a few rappers, however, did it rather well. Among the more notable rap artists and groups were MC Hammer, LL Cool J, Ice-T, Public Enemy, The Beastie Boys, and Run-DMC.†

Mainstream rock during the eighties was made up of several different styles. The driving, straight-ahead rock sounds of bands like Styx, REO Speedwagon, and Huey Lewis & the News were among the most popular. Other bands opted for a tighter, "more produced" sound, as was the case with Talking Heads, Dire Straits, and INXS. A more relaxed, understated, lighter type of rock was popularized by groups such as U2 and R.E.M.

At the same time, the use of synthesizers and/or drum machines had become increasingly common and made up an important part of the music of Phil Collins, Peter Gabriel, Yes, and other groups— not to mention Madonna, Michael Jackson, rap music, and a whole variety of dance styles which had grown quite popular by this time.

---

* The longevity of CDs has never been completely determined. Some say a disk should last about 20 years or so. Others say more, while still others say less. Also, many die-hard vinyl fans are fanatical about their records and swear that the old-fashioned vinyl disks provide superior frequency response and better overall sound quality. To each his own.

† For a wide selection of funk and rap-like grooves, refer to my *Funk Bass, Funk Fusion Bass* and *Bass Grooves: The Ultimate Collection* books.

Sting released his *Dream of the Blue Turtles* and *Nothing Like the Sun* collections, both of which were well received. Pink Floyd (whose *Dark Side of the Moon* seemed like it would stay on the album charts forever) released *The Wall,* a powerful piece of eighties rock history.

Guitar-oriented groups have always been a big part of rock 'n' roll, and the eighties were no exception. Among the most popular guitar bands during the eighties were Journey, ZZ Top, the Traveling Wilburys (featuring George Harrison, Jeff Lynne, Roy Orbison, Bob Dylan, and Tom Petty), and many other groups. Some of the long-established groups, like Santana, Rush, Aerosmith, the Rolling Stones, the J. Geils Band, and the Allman Brothers Band were still going strong, too.

Probably the most significant and most influential type of rock during the eighties was heavy metal. Often accompanied by big hair, spandex, smoke-filled stages, and elaborate light shows, playing to sold-out crowds in arenas holding tens of thousands of screaming music lovers, heavy metal was definitely a major force in 1980s rock 'n' roll. The music was nearly always guitar-based, with plenty of distortion and overdrive. At times, it seemed as though it was more of a culture than a musical style. Among the more popular metal groups of the eighties were Metallica, Def Leppard, Guns N' Roses, Iron Maiden, Mötley Crüe, Cinderella, the Scorpions, Anthrax, Judas Priest, Megadeth, Quiet Riot, Ratt, Skid Row, Whitesnake, AC/DC, Ozzy Osbourne, Tesla, Bon Jovi, Van Halen, and many others.

The list of prominent bass players continued to grow. Among the better known rock bassists of the eighties were Tony Levin, Billy Sheehan, Michael Anthony, Cliff Burton, Nikki Sixx, Mike Mills, Sting, Mark King, Garry Tallent, Tina Weymouth, Pino Palladino, Cliff Williams, Duff McKagan, and many others.

THE GROOVES

This chapter contains a cross-section of the rock styles from the eighties. Listen to the CD to make sure you understand the concepts and play with the proper feel. The discography will be a big help, too. All set? Let's rock on!

Techno-Pop. Grooves 4.1 through 4.5 are indicative of the clean, precise type of rock that was such an integral part of the eighties. The music, with elements of techno-pop, often made use of drum machines, synthesizers, and other electronic gadgets.

Steady Eighth Notes. As a follow-up to the hard rock of the seventies, the driving force of steady eighth-note lines became almost cliché in the eighties. More and more often, repeated eighth notes served as the foundation for the rock music of this decade. Distortion and delay were prime factors too. Grooves 4.6 through 4.9 provide a variety of eighth-note rock grooves.

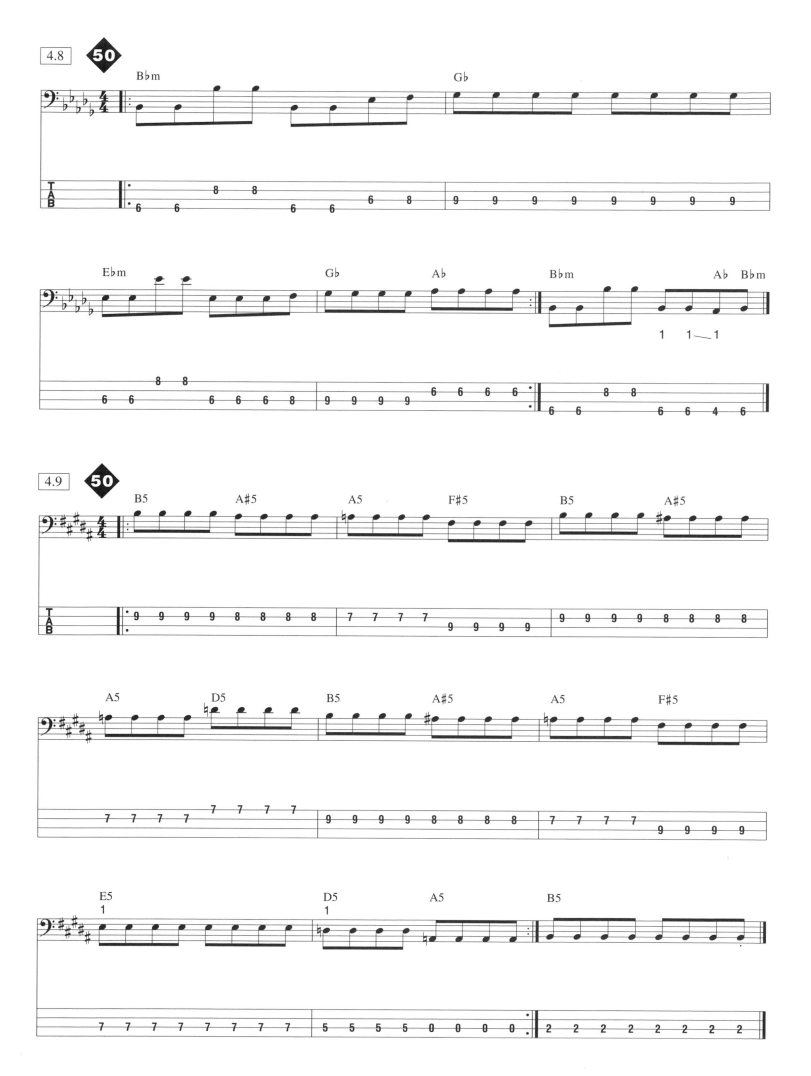

The Power Ballad. Another rock development that became quite popular in the eighties was the "power ballad." Groove 4.10 is an example of this style. Notice, repeated eighth-note patterns were prominent at slower tempos as well.

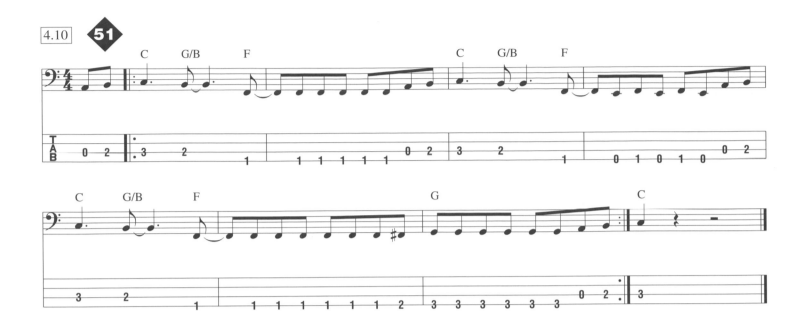

Swing/Shuffle. Though the eighth-note subdivision had clearly become the dominant force in rock, people never seemed to mind hearing an occasional shuffle amidst all their other favorite grooves. Groove 4.11 is an example of an eighties rock shuffle. The general feel is basically the same as earlier shuffle grooves. The line is just a little less traditional in the way it jumps from one register to another and in the placement of the accents.

Heavy Metal. Grooves 4.12 through 4.18 illustrate different examples of heavy metal rock 'n' roll. Pay close attention to the attack as you concentrate on the drum beats, the use of the guitar, and the overall attitude. Think: arena rock!

"Welcome to the Jungle..."

By the end of the eighties, rock 'n' roll had continued to veer off in many directions. There was now diversity begetting diversity. The result was a situation whereby the coexistence of countless subcultures was creating more and more variety. Even the way music was conceptualized, performed, and recorded had changed dramatically. Completely-outfitted home studios—with synthesizers, sequencers, drum machines, and samplers—had become the norm. Musicians now had the ability to do more with less.

Yet, amidst all this diversity, a common bond still existed, an imaginary thread that could be traced back to the roots shared by all of the rock cultures. The Rock and Roll Hall of Fame was being formalized. A list of inductees of rock legends dating all the way back to the beginning of rock was being compiled, years before the Hall of Fame building, in Cleveland, Ohio, was even built.

As the eighties drew to a close, many yuppies (young urban professionals) assumed a "What have we done?!" attitude. People who had been consumed by the glamour that the eighties had brought, those who had become caught in the heat of the moment, were coming to the realization that you can't get "something for nothing" and that "there ain't no such thing as a free lunch." The realization became more apparent as they watched more individuals going to jail for Wall Street crimes, including junk bond trading and inside information scandals. The eighties were over. The world, once again, was eager for change.

'90s

The '90s

POLITICS AND CULTURE

Life in the nineties was never without its share of adversity, conflict, strife, and controversy. In 1990, a civil war erupted in Yugoslavia, launching a bloody battle of nationalism and ethnic hatred among Serbs, Croats, and Muslims. In the Soviet Union, an unsuccessful coup by communist hardliners set the stage for the breakup of the communist party in Russia, ousting Mikhail Gorbachev as premier and bringing Boris Yeltsin to power. Around the same time, Iraq's Saddam Hussein was invading Kuwait, inciting the United States to lead a coalition of more than two dozen nations against Iraq in the Persian Gulf War. The Republic of South Africa held its first majority rule election in which Nelson Mandela was named president of that nation after having served nearly thirty years in a white South African prison due to his political beliefs.

In the United States, radical groups such as the Ku Klux Klan, Neo-Nazis, Skinheads, various militia groups, cults, foreign governments, and other organizations made themselves known through various acts of violence and self-destruction. Explosions rocked the World Trade Center in New York City and the Alfred P. Murrah Federal Building in Oklahoma City. Tragic incidents took the lives of loyal followers of the cults of David Koresh in Waco, Texas and Heaven's Gate in California, the latter incident being all too reminiscent of the Jonestown Massacre, nearly two decades earlier.

Voters in California passed Proposition 187, cutting off education and social services for illegal aliens. For nearly a year, the world became obsessed with the trial of former football star O.J. Simpson, who ultimately was acquitted in the murders of his former wife, Nicole Brown Simpson, and her friend, Ronald Goldman. The United States and Russia worked side by side in the Mir Space Station, miles above planet earth. Even the tobacco companies admitted that smoking may be harmful to your health!

Meanwhile, the world had become enamored with the concept of global communication. Car phones, beepers, fax machines, and voice mail were all commonplace—it was not out of the ordinary to see people talking on cellular phones on the street, in the grocery store, or on the stair-stepping machine at the gym. The masses, particularly those under thirty (and in many cases, much younger), had fallen in love with e-mail, the World Wide Web, and "surfing the Internet."

Included among the hit movies of the nineties were *Basic Instinct, The Shawshank Redemption, Jurassic Park, Pulp Fiction,* and *Jerry Maguire.* The *Star Wars* trilogy also enjoyed a twenty-year anniversary release, much to the delight of both young and old. TV viewers enjoyed watching "Seinfeld," "Married with Children," "Melrose Place," and "E.R." MTV's Beavis and Butthead became the top pop icons of the decade. One interesting milestone in American culture occurred when millions saw Ellen DeGeneres's character "come out" on the "Ellen" show, informing the world that she was a lesbian; society had come a long way since Mary Tyler Moore made history a quarter century earlier by showing the public that it was socially acceptable for a single woman to live on her own and be self-supporting.

Volvos and BMWs had given way to Jeep Cherokees, mini-vans, and sport utility vehicles. The hero of anti-establishment corporate America was Dilbert.

Freedom of expression had reached an all-time high in the nineties, culminating in an "anything goes" attitude. Various types of tattoos seemed to be growing more and more popular, as did body piercing (including multiple earrings, lip rings, tongue, nose, nipple, and you-name-it rings). Never-ending creativity continued to flourish with regard to hair styles and clothing, including torn jeans, flannel shirts, and very, *very* baggy pants.

MUSIC

Rock 'n' roll was still alive and well in the nineties. The Rock and Roll Hall of Fame opened its 150,000 square foot museum in Cleveland, some dozen years after that organization's formation. The inductees to the Hall of Fame, which by this time numbered approximately one hundred, now had a home where they could be recognized and appreciated for their efforts and contributions. MTV introduced its "unplugged" series, which featured acoustic reworkings of old material from Eric Clapton, Neil Young,

Rod Stewart, Led Zeppelin, and many other acts. Even Nirvana and Kiss were on the "unplugged" list. In 1994, a Woodstock festival was staged in commemoration of the original happening's twenty-fifth anniversary. The performers included everyone from Bob Dylan to Nine Inch Nails and the Red Hot Chili Peppers.

During the nineties, the music world continued to serve up a wide variety of rock 'n' roll. Some of the more pop-oriented artists included Bryan Adams, Gloria Estefan (and her Miami Sound Machine), and Sting. Among the relative newcomers to the scene were Bush, Mariah Carey, Sheryl Crow, Hootie & the Blowfish, and the Dave Matthews Band.

As rock music continued to become more and more diversified, the distinctions between different types of rock, primarily "metal" and "hard rock," were often blurred. Another term that people seemed to fall in love with in the nineties was "alternative." Bands that got classified as alternative often overlapped into the rock and heavy metal categories as well. Alternative music had no specific rules or parameters. It was not radically different from traditional or mainstream rock 'n' roll—just played with a different attitude, which reflected the styles of the time. Alternative bands were often guitar-based, making frequent use of repetitive eighth-note figures and a driving backbeat. The music could make use of distortion and effects or opt for a clean or acoustic sound. Among the artists and groups generally considered alternative were Alanis Morissette, Smashing Pumpkins, Green Day, the Gin Blossoms, the Goo Goo Dolls, the Stone Temple Pilots, Beck, the Cranberries, and others.

Many of the "older" artists from previous decades still enjoyed fame and success in the nineties. Included in this group were Phil Collins, Eric Clapton, Tom Petty, Elton John, Pink Floyd, and U2. Music lovers delighted in seeing the reunions of Kiss and the Eagles. Especially noteworthy was the enormous success of the Beatles *Anthology* series (video and CD compilations) which, to the surprise of many, proved that the Fab Four were actually more popular in the nineties than they were in their heyday, more than thirty years earlier! What's more, several groups, including Oasis and Crowded House, built their sound on sixties-style rock 'n' roll, paying tribute to the Beatles-era genre.

Hard rock and heavy metal continued as strong as ever in the nineties. Among the groups in this category were Metallica, White Zombie, the Red Hot Chili Peppers, Guns N' Roses, Rage Against the Machine, and Nine Inch Nails.

Perhaps the most important development in rock 'n' roll during the nineties was the "grunge" movement, formed in the Pacific Northwest. Seattle was the place where this new style was launched, through the efforts of Nirvana, Pearl Jam, Soundgarden, Alice In Chains, and others. Grunge was, for the most part, the next phase in the progression from hard rock to heavy metal. The music was guitar-based and had strong metal influences and simple, singable melodies. It could be loud and raucous as well as soft and, well, "unplugged."

Naturally, the nineties offered us a new generation of rock bass players (or a higher profile to some of the already established ones). Among the more prominent bassists of the nineties were Jason Newsted, Krist Novoselic, Jeff Ament, Les Claypool, Flea, MeShell NdegéOcello, Dave Ellefson, Ben Shepherd, Trent Reznor, and many others.

THE GROOVES

Overall, rock in the nineties remained loyal to its musical roots. You still hear plenty of blues-based tunes from this decade, an occasional shuffle, hard rock and metal influences, and everything in between. Here I have presented you with a cross-section of nineties-style rock 'n' roll. Make sure you've moved your time machine forward and made the appropriate attitude adjustments.

Combining Elements. Much of the music of the nineties had an understated quality. Though it's played with plenty of conviction, at the same time, it's a bit laid back. Sometimes variations of sixteenth-note patterns are used to create a sort of bouncy feel, especially when played with a quasi hip-hop drum beat. Repeated eighth-note figures, more or less a carryover from the eighties, are quite common. Straight-ahead, hard-driving grooves make up a big part of the music of this decade, though they contain certain "twists" to keep the music sounding fresh. In most cases, the grooves are derived from a combination of all these elements. Try playing selections 5.1 through 5.12. The CD will help you get the right feel.

58

Odd Time Signatures. How about a few odd time signatures? Count *very* carefully!

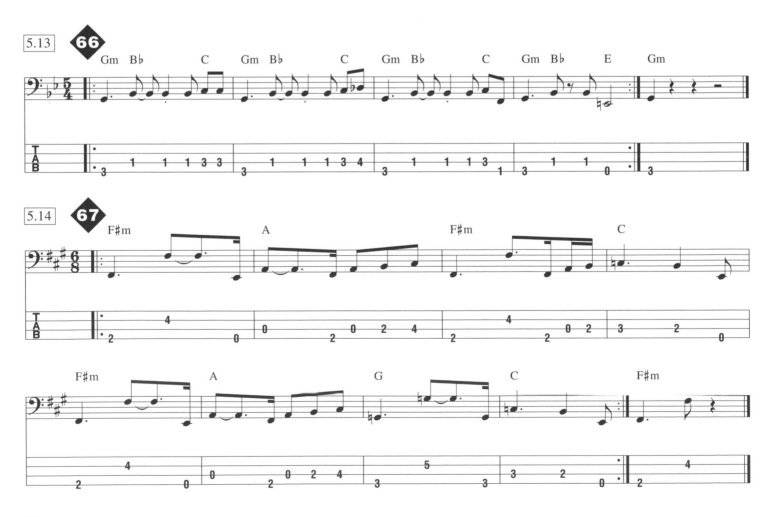

Grunge. Much of the hard rock and metal-oriented music developed a harder edge to it, often with a touch of anger. At times, the voice leading was more angular and jagged, further adding to the tension. The following grooves start out with sort of a post-hard rock/post-heavy metal feel, then culminate in an all-out grunge party! I think you'll enjoy these.

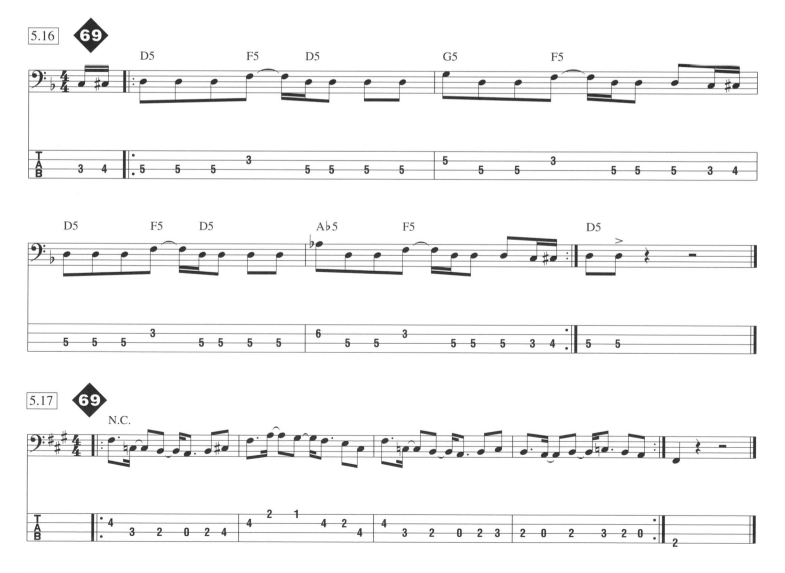

"What Would You Say...?"

So, what do you think Elvis Presley or Buddy Holly would think if they could experience the state of rock 'n' roll so many years after they had each made their mark? And who's to say what's next? Well, far be it from me to speculate.

However…

Anyone who's studied the history of rock 'n' roll should recognize certain trends and common ingredients that have remained fairly constant, practically from the beginning. A driving, eighth-note feel has been fairly consistent, at least since the late fifties. The strong backbeat has always been an integral part of rock 'n' roll. Shuffle grooves, though not as much a part of the norm, have always had an important and special place throughout every decade in rock history. All of these components have withstood the test of time and continue to be important elements of rock 'n' roll today. The guitar, always a major force in rock 'n' roll, does not seem to be in danger of becoming extinct any time soon. Young people still have that natural tendency to rebel, which always makes for some interesting music. As hair and clothing styles come and go, all of these other factors have, for the most part, remained constant and are likely to continue so into the future.

Technology has come a long way since the 1950s and continues to progress at a frenetic pace. Synthesizers and computer-based music are likely to retain an important role in rock music as well. Some say that styles such as electro, house, breakbeat, drum-and-bass, trip-hop, and other forms of techno-pop will become the mainstream music of the day. On the other hand, perhaps the popularity of the unplugged series is indicative of rock returning to its roots by saying "what's old is what's new."

The world has changed so much, even since the first edition of this book was published. The 9/11 terrorist attacks, the U.S. invasion of Iraq and the subsequent captures of Saddam Hussein and Osama bin Laden have transformed the world forever. The use of social media has revolutionized the way we communicate, through the use of Facebook, YouTube, Twitter and many other platforms. Apple's breakthrough iPod, iPhone and other products have become true "game changers" in the daily lives of millions of people throughout the world. Barack Obama became the first African American President of the United States and Britain's Queen Elizabeth II celebrated her Diamond Jubilee. Scientists have discovered water on the moon and civilian space travel is becoming a reality.

All the while, the music continues. Many long-established rock acts, including Paul McCartney, the Rolling Stones, Yes, Rush, Aerosmith, Metallica and several others continue to perform and tour, exhibiting seemingly endless energy and endurance (not to mention the surviving members of Led Zeppelin's on again/off again talks of a reunion).

As in the past, art and music will respond to the social climate. Here, at the dawn of the new millennium, what lies in store for us is anybody's guess. One thing that remains fairly certain though is that rock 'n' roll is here to stay.

Long live rock!

Building a Vocabulary for Rock Soloing

In all of my books, I have emphasized the groove and stressed the necessity of being able to groove with a great time feel. In most cases, a groove is a pattern intended to be played over and over again, along with the drummer, to set up a foundation over which the rest of the music is built. In some cases, the music calls for the bassist to repeat a passage countless times, with little or no variation, creating a hypnotic, almost religious experience. The groove sets the mood, the feeling, the vibe, whatever you want to call it. Never underestimate the importance of the groove.

Sometimes, though, we bassists get to step out from the role of being strictly supportive and get to have the band support *us* for a change. The concept of "bass solo" (sometimes referred to as, *"Oh, no — bass solo!"*) has never been as common as that of guitar solo, keyboard solo, saxophone solo, or even drum solo. But it does have a place in rock music, especially with all the great rock bass players we have today.

In *Rock Bass*, as in my other books, I have devoted an entire chapter to the art of soloing. As always, I must give my disclaimer: Your job is to groove. Soloing is nice, but it's not your primary function. The selections in this chapter are intended to give you ideas for developing rock bass solos. They will provide you with a wide variety of licks commonly used in rock 'n' roll. But remember: when your solo is over, it's over. At that time, you need to get back to taking care of business, which in almost every case means keeping it simple!

I think you'll have fun with these licks. They are not indicative of any particular decade of rock 'n' roll so you'll be able to adapt them to many different musical situations. Though each lick has a repeat sign, these licks are generally not intended to be repeated as grooves. I wrote them as grooves so they will be easier to learn and to master. You can actually groove on every one of them! The idea, though, is to familiarize yourself with different rock styles and try to come up with licks (and grooves!) of your own. You might even want to try developing your own lines by combining several of these licks. The variety of keys will make this process a bit challenging, but transposing and playing in different keys is good for you! Remember to refer to the CD to hear the proper interpretations.

Ready. Set. Bass solo!

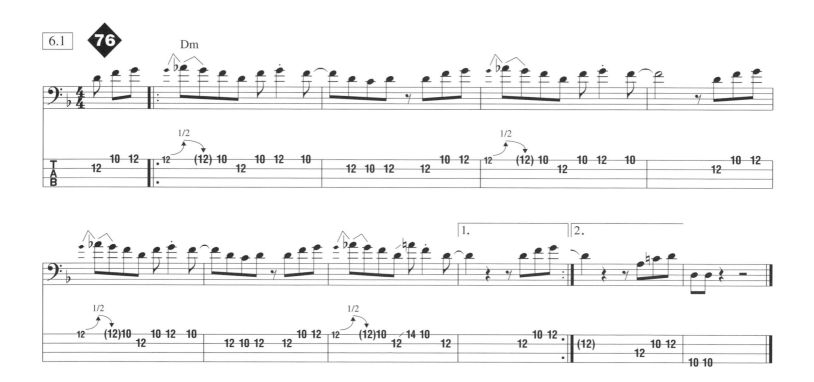

APPENDIX:
YOUR EQUIPMENT AND EFFECTS

Trying to sort through the overwhelming amount of equipment and effects available to musicians today can really make your head spin. What's more, all the letters, numbers, symbols, and acronyms make the whole process sound like alphabet soup. How are you supposed to know what all of these gadgets do, and how do you decide what you really need?

The purpose of this appendix is to enlighten the contemporary bass player, *in plain English,* so that he or she can sift intelligently through the incredible number of music products available on the market and cope more easily with the ever-changing technology that faces musicians today. The aspects dealt within these pages include choosing an instrument, strings, amplifiers, speakers, and effects—taking into account the particular needs of today's rock bassist.

Though I can offer you information, the choices are ultimately yours. The best thing to do is experiment. Listen to the music I have included in the discography. See what you can find in iTunes, Spotify, Pandora and YouTube. Decide just what sound it is you're going for, then try to achieve that sound. Read the trade magazines, like *Bass Player* and see who's into what. You can find a wealth of information online, too, particularly on www.ForBassPlayersOnly.com and other websites. Look at the ads. Hang out in music stores. Check things out. Talk to the guys (and girls) who play the way you'd like to play and find out how they set up their basses, what strings they use and what kinds of effects they like (or don't like).

Sometimes on a recording, they'll list the equipment used. Watch for these kinds of things, too. Don't allow yourself to be too heavily influenced by product endorsements though. Only buy something because *you* like it, not because your favorite rock star advocates its use.*

Keep your eyes and ears open. Somebody is always coming out with "the latest thing." Try to emulate the "in" sound as much as possible so people will know you're hip, but at the same time, put a little of yourself into your sound, so people will know you're unique.

Make sure you look around long and hard enough to buy intelligently. These days, it's very easy to get product reviews online, too, which can be a big help. I always feel better buying name-brand equipment with some kind of warranty. Once you decide what you want, shop around for the best deal. Competition is fierce among music stores. Always try to buy from a reputable dealer who's been around for a long time and won't give you any hassles if something goes wrong. If you have to buy used equipment, check out the person first, and make sure everything smells "kosher" before you give your money to anyone. Take your time, and explore your options. Good luck.

YOUR BASS

With so many types of basses available, you'll have to explore many options when considering what type of instrument to buy and what features are important to you. It used to be simple: years ago, you went out and bought a Fender "Jazz" or a Fender "Precision" bass and an amp (probably an Ampeg B-15), and you had everything you needed because that's all there was! (OK, maybe I'm exaggerating a little, but not that much.)

Nowadays, we've still got Fenders, but we've also got guys like Michael Tobias, Ken Smith, Jerzy Drozd, Christian Noguera and several others who know everything there is to know about every type of wood in the world, from ebony, rosewood and maple to alder, Pernambuco and bubinga. They know which type of tree from which tropical rain forest in Brazil will make the best neck for getting the most sustain out of a bass when cut in just the right way (this time, I'm *not* exaggerating!). We've also got Alembic, Aria, B.C. Rich, Carvin, Clevinger, Conklin, Dingwall, Epiphone, ESP, Fernandes, Fodera, G&L, Hamer, Hofner, Hohner, Ibanez, Kubicki, Lakland, Little, Modulus, Music Man, Peavey, Pedulla, Pensa, Rickenbacker, Sadowsky, Samick, Schecter, Skjold, Spector, Steinberger, Tune, Wal, Warwick, Washburn, Yamaha, Zeta, Zon and so many others.

---

* Book endorsements are OK, though!

Some basses have solid bodies, while others are hollow. We've got bolt-on necks and through-the-body necks. We've even got graphite necks. In addition to the four-, five- and six-string basses to which we've all grown accustomed, basses today can have seven, nine, eleven or virtually any number of strings you can imagine. You can find basses that are fretted, fretless or half-and-half. For the technically inclined, we've even got MIDI basses from Industrial Radio, Manne, Godin and several others. Like most things, choosing a bass comes down to three things: 1) What do you like; 2) What do you need; and 3) What can you afford?

Pickups. Choosing the right pickups for your bass is crucial for attaining your desired sound. Understanding the concept of how pickups work is easy. Deciding on and purchasing just the right pickup can be quite a challenge. "Under the hood" of each pickup is, basically, just a wire wrapped around a magnet. There are many different pickup manufacturers today, not to mention a whole bunch of pickup buzzwords and jargon. When you come right down to it, though, no matter how many pickups you scrutinize, most will be variations on this same (admittedly oversimplified) theme.

The most basic is the *single coil* pickup, which is made by wrapping a single wire around a magnet. A *humbucking* pickup is made from two single coils placed next to each other in opposite directions, in order to eliminate the hum that frequently occurs due to interference from the amplifier or some other external force. Many variations exist with regard to the number of times the wire is wrapped around the magnets, precise placement against the strings, etc.

Pickups are said to be either active or passive. Passive pickups are, technologically, very simple. They allow the signal to pass through their circuitry without altering its natural sound. Active pickups, on the other hand, are not only used to help amplify the signal, but, with the aid of a power source (in most cases, a 9-volt battery), they can dramatically alter the sound of your bass by varying the frequency response and equalization. Active pickups are extremely versatile and have grown enormously popular.

Most pickups come in either a "J" (for "Jazz" Bass) or a "P-J" ("Precision/Jazz") configuration. The P-J set-up is a hybrid configuration, taking the best of both worlds from the twin pickups on a Jazz bass and the single pickup on a Precision bass. This arrangement keeps the single Precision-style pickup near the center of the body and adds a Jazz-style pickup close to the bridge. This variation allows more high frequencies to pass, as well as more overall sound flexibility. "Soapbar" is another popular pickup design. It gets its name from its shape and could contain any of a number of pickup configurations and electronics. Some high-quality pick-ups include Bartolini, Dean Markley, DiMarzio, Gibson, Joe Barden, Ken Smith, Lindy Fralin, Nordstrand, Schaller, Sadowsky, Seymour Duncan and several others. Don't forget to change that little 9-volt battery every once in a while in the pick-ups that need it.

The Bridge. Proper bridge selection is extremely important for sustain, spacing, action, and calibration. Maybe you've just got to have a whammy bar. That's OK, too. Most bridges are made of silver plated brass, which is an excellent material for sustain. Some popular manufacturers of bridges include Badass (Leo Quan), Full Contact Hardware, Gotoh, Hipshot, Kahler, Schaller and others. On many bridges, the saddles are adjustable, so you can vary the spacing between strings. Others must have slots cut into them to secure the strings. These slots are permanent, so make sure whoever cuts the bridge for you knows what he or she is doing.

Many times a bridge will require a tiny *Allen* wrench to adjust the action (height) of each string and a small screwdriver to adjust the calibration (horizontal movement of the saddle) to be sure the bass plays in tune. Unless you want to end up using your nail clippers, make sure you always carry the right tools with you. You never know when your band might get a big gig in some Third World country, and you don't feel like braving the town on your own looking for a hardware store. (Take it from me, it happens!)

Tuning Machines and Nut. Hang on, we're not done yet. Make sure your bass has good quality tuning machines that won't get stuck, turn too hard, or slip. Fender, Grover, Hipshot, Mighty Mite, Modulus, Schaller, Sperzel and several other companies make popular tuning machines. Another important consideration is the nut (the slotted piece of hardware at the top of the neck that secures the strings between the fingerboard and the head). Don't overlook this little device. It's an important part of the bass and can significantly affect the overall tone. Nuts come in brass, ebony, graphite, bone—even plastic. (Don't buy a plastic nut!) Make sure the nut is the right size for your bass and has the proper spacing between the slots. In some cases, the slots may need to be filed down. Make sure whoever files down the nut is qualified, because if it's filed too low, it will need to be replaced.

So what's the best instrument to use for playing rock bass? Since everyone is different, I can't tell you; I can only guide you. Do you have an aggressive attack, or are you a soft touch? Do you like to slap and pop a lot? Does your band play a lot of Nirvana tunes, or is Don Ho more your thing?

The type of bass that's best for you will depend on the type of player you are and the circumstances in which you're playing. For example, it is not at all uncommon for a studio bassist to take four or five basses, or even more, to a session. On the other hand, a prolonged, intense tour of successive one-nighters probably won't afford a bassist the luxury of taking more than one or two basses, so he or she must choose carefully.

Does your music lend itself more to the sound of a "traditional" four-string bass, or would a five- or six-string be more appropriate? Many five- and six-string basses have very narrow spacing between the strings to avoid having to make the neck too wide. Steinberger is one extreme. Ken Smith, on the other hand, who maintains the four-string spacing on his five- and six-string basses (which have *super-wide* necks) is one exception. I bought a couple of "fives" during that whole craze back in the eighties. Truth is, somehow I gravitated back to a "four" almost exclusively. Four strings seem "gutsier" to me for some reason. Like everything else, it's a matter of personal taste, as well as what is the most appropriate sound for the music you're playing.

YOUR STRINGS

The next thing you'll need is a good set of strings for your bass. A great many types of strings are available today, so you'll really have to do some experimenting in this department. Flatwound strings, made from nickel- or chrome-plated steel, are still widely available, but are not as popular as roundwounds. Some people prefer flatwounds, finding them more comfortable than roundwounds. Flatwounds tend to be quieter, too, making less finger noise. A lot of fretless players like flatwounds as they tend to be easier on the neck than roundwounds.

Roundwound strings, on the other hand, produce a much brighter and crisper sound. They feel rougher than flatwounds because of the round, stainless steel wire and the grooves along the outer core. Bass strings can be flatwounds, roundwounds or a combination of the two. String gauge is important, too. Most rockers prefer strings gauged toward the heavier side (say, .045, .065, .085, and .105, or heavier). You may decide you like something within this range, or maybe something all the way to one extreme or the other. Again, it's up to you.

Not only do strings come in a million different gauges, but they also come in short scale, medium scale, long scale, and double-ball end (for the Steinbergers and copies). Make sure you get the right type of strings for your bass, and always *(do yourself a favor!), always* carry spare sets with you. If you aren't always able to have a new set of strings on deck, save the old ones when you take them off. They just might save your life one night.

It could take a long time to experiment with the wide variety of strings that are available today. And with all the different manufacturers, gauges, configurations, tone nuances, and other considerations, the process could get somewhat expensive. Go to a music store, and try several basses with different types of strings. Try your friends' basses. Make more friends, and try their basses. Take a chance once in a while and try something new. Be bold! Be daring!

Throughout your quest for the ultimate string, keep in mind that you're seeking the strings that sound the best and last the longest. Some string manufacturers you should be aware of include D'Addario, Dean Markley, DR, Dunlop, Elixir, Ernie Ball, Fender, GHS, La Bella, Lakland, MTD, Pedulla, Rotosound, Sadowsky and S.I.T., to name but a few.

YOUR AMPLIFIER AND SPEAKERS

What do you want your amplifier to do? Do you want it to just make you louder? Do you want it to embellish or otherwise modify your sound? Do you want it to *make* your sound? Do you want it to *be* your sound? Are 50 watts enough? Are 1300 watts enough? What kind of speakers should you use? Do those Bose four-inchers do the trick for you? Maybe you'd like one of those gigantic Ampeg 8 X 10 cabinets. Or how about an SWR 18-inch "Goliath" woofer?

Here we are, facing still more choices. The best advice I can give you is, first, don't skimp on quality; and second, though you can allow a little room for growth, only get what you really need. Overnight sensations are few and far between. Most people who rise to the top do it one step at a time.

Amplifiers. Bass amps have just about any features you could want these days. Many have built-in equalizers for the ultimate in frequency manipulation. Others have internal compression and limiting capabilities. Many amps have direct outputs (for direct boxes and house systems), effects sends, and outputs for recording. Outputs could be for standard quarter-inch plugs or for balanced XLR connectors. Most amps are mono, though stereo amps do exist. It's also possible to combine two or more amps together to achieve a stereo effect, provided your bass is wired for stereo. Even if it's not, there are ways to simulate a stereo effect through proper configuring of signal processors. (For more on the technical aspects, see the section on effects.)

Older amps contained tubes that necessitated a waiting period as they heated up. As technology progressed, the newer amps were "solid-state," built with transistors instead of tubes. This design allowed the bassist to plug in, turn on, and play—*now.* But as time went on, many purists found that the tube amps delivered a cleaner, more natural sound and that they preferred them over solid-state amps. (These are probably the same people that prefer vinyl records to CDs.) Nowadays, both tube and solid-state amps are available. Once again, what's old is what's new.

Your amp should have at least 100 watts of power. Granted, that level is not very high by today's standards, but in most cases it's all you'll need. If you need more, you can find amps with 1,000 watts of power, or even more. The sky's the limit! You don't have to go overboard, though. I've performed at Madison Square Garden and the Shrine Auditorium with 400-watt amps (going through the house systems, of course).

As far as amp settings go, there are about as many ways to configure those knobs as there are knob configurers. Everyone has his or her own personal taste for setting the low, midrange, and high frequencies, and certain sounds have come to be expected. (Many people, for example, not only like to hear the bass, but to *feel* it too, and adjust the low-range frequencies accordingly.) Don't forget all the other variables that go into producing the sound, like the player, the bass, strings, effects (we'll get to them in a minute), and speakers. Many other important factors exist in determining your settings. Are you playing inside or outside? Are you in a big room or a small one? Is the room full or empty? Does the room have a high ceiling? Wooden floors? Carpeting? Is it a "dead" room or a "live" room? You've got to consider everything and act accordingly.

Lots of great amps are out on the market these days. SWR and Gallien-Krueger are quite popular. Trace-Elliot makes some fantastic amps, too. Some people like Walter Woods amps, while others are partial to Acoustic or Peavey. You should also check out Accugroove, Aguilar, Ampeg, Ashdown, Carvin, Crate, Eden, Epifani, Fender, Genz-Benz, Gibson, Hartke (Samson), Hughes & Kettner, Line 6, Markbass, Marshall, Mesa-Boogie, Orange, Pearce, Polytone, Randall, Sunn, TC Electronic, Warwick, Yamaha and more.

Speakers. The speaker you use with your amp can make or break your rig. I wasn't kidding when I mentioned four-inch speakers for bass. The Bose 802s are made up of eight 4.5-inch speakers per cabinet, and some bass players (mostly upright players) swear by them. I wouldn't recommend them for our purposes here, but if you want to try them, maybe you'll like them! Electro-Voice and JBL still make great speakers and will probably be around forever. Hartke and SWR cabinets have become enormously popular over the years. I definitely wouldn't buy a speaker before testing them. You should also check out Aguilar, Eminence, Fender, Genz-Benz, Markbass, Marshall, Mesa Boogie, Peavy and TC Electronic. Many more are available, too. Check them all out!

Now let's take a look at some speaker types and sizes. It's important to make your bass sound good in all registers. You need that low, boomy (but not *too* boomy) tone on the bottom, and that extra crispness and percussiveness at the top. You'll also need a certain amount of midrange to add some body.

So what kind of speaker(s) will give us that ultimate bass sound in all registers from rock-bottom "B" to stratosphere "C?" Start experimenting! Bass speaker technology is about as sophisticated as you could want. Try bi-amping or tri-amping. Or just use a 12-inch speaker in a good cabinet. Or how about four 10-inch speakers. I had a cabinet built once with a 15-inch JBL speaker and a horn, which I liked very much.

Some companies, like Hartke, SWR and several others, have a variety of speaker configurations, which can be combined in many ways. Among the most common set-ups are cabinets with either one 15-inch speaker, two 10-inch speakers, or four 10-inch speakers. Many bassists, like Will Lee and Darryl Jones, get a large part of their sound by using different combinations of these three configurations.

SWR's "Goliath" line has a feature I've always liked, where there is a "bullet" placed amid the speakers, controlled by a knob in the back of the cabinet. The knob can turn the bullet completely off, completely on or anywhere in between. It's very practical for adjusting the high-end frequencies, giving your bass some extra punch.

YOUR EFFECTS

Well, what do you like and what do you *need?* It's all out there, folks. It's very easy to go overboard in this department, and in fact, many people do. Don't get caught up in the arms race to see who can accumulate the biggest, deadliest, most "awesome" arsenal of toys. People who think along those lines are missing the point. Signal processors are wonderful tools available to *embellish* our sound. Remember, though, they are the means, not the end.

Following is a list of effects, devices, and gadgets that are common in music today, and a brief description of each one. Of course, words alone are not sufficient for describing these effects (it would be like *telling* you what Stuart Hamm or Billy Sheehan sounded like without you ever having had the chance to hear them!), so make sure you get your hands (and ears) on them for yourself, and do lots of experimenting. Many more types of effects are available, but the ones here are among the most common.

Volume Pedal. Let's start with an easy one. Volume pedals are great for controlling the strength of the signal going into your amp, when you just can't stop playing, not even for an eighth note. They also allow you to play more expressively. Some run on batteries, some have AC power cords, and others require no external power source at all. Many volume pedals are coupled with a "wah-wah" effect. Test out your volume pedal before you buy it, and make sure it feels comfortable, moves smoothly, and is sensitive (but not *too* sensitive) to subtle movements. Also, it should have some kind of rubber feet or "stoppers" on the bottom to keep it from sliding around while you play. Most pedals do, but in case yours doesn't, or if they fall off (and they *do* fall off!), be prepared to put a towel or whatever else you can improvise under your pedal to keep it secure and to keep you from losing your mind. Most volume pedals run about $60 to $75 and up. Once you start using one, you'll wonder how you ever got along without it.

Tuner. Not really an effect, but your music will sound more effective if you play in tune. A quartz tuner is a very handy device to have. It allows you to plug your bass directly into a little box and then shows you if you're in tune, sharp or flat, even if you can't actually hear yourself. (Try asking everyone in the room to be quiet for a minute so you can tune your bass, and see what kind of reaction you get!) Just about everybody has a tuner on the market. They typically sell for less than $100, often quite a bit less. You don't always get what you pay for, though, so be careful. I once purchased one of the "better" quartz tuners and found it to be about ten cents sharp.

Most tuners have a little condenser microphone that picks up sounds that are in the air. This feature is handy for singers, woodwind and brass players, etc. Also, many tuners allow you to change the "reference" pitch from A-440 to, say, A-442 or even A-445.

When playing music, especially in the studio, there's a big difference between playing in tune and playing *incredibly* in tune. Some studios are equipped with strobe tuners which are even more accurate than quartz tuners. Keep in mind, though, that the tuner is just a tool and a guide. Although technology has come a long way and we have "super-accurate" tuners at our disposal, your *ear* is always the final judge.

OK, ready to get down to the good stuff? Just be careful you don't overdo it and get in over your head—especially when the guy at the music store, or the geek down the block, tells you you've got to have a GTX/280Z-50 or you're just not with it. Effects are important. They're just more important to some people than to others. On the one hand, we have players like Steve Swallow and Victor Bailey, who use little or no effects and depend on their hands to get their sound (what a concept!). On the other hand, we've got guys like Mark Egan who owns at least one of everything! Each piece of equipment Mark has, though, was acquired for a specific reason, because he knows what he's doing and he's constantly thinking of "the big picture." What sound(s) are you going for, and how will each variable in your chain of processors affect your overall sound? If you've just gotta have a GTX/280Z-50, so be it!

In most cases, the effects described below are available either in rack-mountable modules or "stomp boxes" (pedals that are turned on and off by stepping on them). Virtually all of them are available in mono, stereo, or "simulated stereo." Guitar and bass players have traditionally favored the stomp boxes over the rack-mounts, but that trend may be changing. The rack-mounts are often less noisy, and in most cases, of higher quality than the stomp boxes. Also, some of the rack-mounts provide several effects at once. Furthermore, through the use of MIDI, parameters, patch changes, and overall sounds can be executed on the rack-mounts via a MIDI foot pedal.

This technology can get expensive, though. What's more, many die-hard guitar players just love their stomp boxes and wouldn't trade them for anything. Like I've said before, it's up to you. Some good quality manufacturers of effects include: Alesis, Aphex, Ashdown, Boss, DBX, Digitech, D.O.D., Electro-Harmonix, Eventide, Furman, Hughes & Kettner, Korg, Lexicon, Line 6, Morley, Rane, Rocktron, Roland, TC Electronic, Tech 21, Yamaha and many others.

Delay. Here's an effect that has grown tremendously popular among bass players over the years, especially for fretlesses. While using a delay, the sound of your bass is reproduced and repeated anywhere from a few milliseconds to several seconds later. Originally, delays were achieved by the old method of using a tape recorder to get a time delay between the "record" and the "playback" heads. Soon afterward, analog, or solid-state, delays came into popular use.

Today, tape and analog delays have given way to digital delays. Digital technology uses an encoding process which interprets audio signals as binary digits (zeros and ones). Digital delays (or DDLs, as we say in the biz) offer extremely clean sound and faithful reproduction at a fraction of the cost.

Chorus. A chorus is a popular effect that can greatly enhance the sound of your bass. This processor electronically delays and varies the pitch of the output signal above and below that of the input signal. As the two signals are blended together, your ear perceives the two sounds as having been made at the same time, thus creating a wavy, multiple-voice effect. Chorusing is best appreciated in stereo, with the processed signal coming out of one speaker and the unprocessed signal out of the other.

Flanger. A flanger is actually another form of modulated delay. It copies the signal, delays it, varies the pitch, and then mixes the delayed signal back with the original signal. The delay time, however, is usually much shorter than in a chorus. What's more, a portion of the processed sound can be redirected back into the input for further processing, resulting in a feedback loop. It is this feedback that gives the flanger its distinctive swishing and whooshing effect. Flanging was originally done with two tape recorders, by increasing and decreasing the speed of one of the reels, while the other remained constant. This technique was known as a "reel flange."

Reverb. Though this effect is not as common among bassists as it is for, well, *everyone* else, it's such a "biggie" in today's sound that it just can't be overlooked. Simply stated, reverb is the perception of the different ways sound bounces off the walls in a room. The larger the room, the greater the echo. (Of course it's a lot more complex, but basically that's the idea.)

Reverb devices can be divided into four basic types: spring, plate, chamber, and (what else?) digital. Spring reverb was the culprit all those times you (and I) bumped the Twin Reverb or the Vocal Master and caused what sounded like an explosion. Plate reverb, once common in recording studios, involved a suspended plate with a transducer in the middle. Chamber reverb was created in a specially designed "acoustic room," often made of concrete or shellacked material, with no parallel walls.

Digital, as you may have guessed, is the most prominent type of reverb used in music today. It is extremely flexible in that it can be configured in an infinite number of ways, by varying the decay time, equalization, crossover points, and all kinds of other really neat technical stuff. Most digital reverb units have memory presets, so you can "call up" your favorite reverb type by pushing a button or two. Your reverb unit will probably have settings called "small hall," "medium hall," "concert hall," etc. Often they get pretty fancy, too, with effects like "reverse reverb," "gated reverb," "reverse gated reverb," and so on. Some of the very intricate digital reverb units in recording studios can simulate spring, plate, and chamber reverbs, as well. (You see, producers always have to have just the right reverb on the snare drum and will usually go to any expense to get it!)

Equalizer. Equalizers are very practical devices to have and can drastically alter your overall sound. An equalizer, or *EQ,* isolates a particular frequency (or range of frequencies) so that it can be either boosted or cut. Basically, EQs come in two types: graphic and parametric. A graphic EQ allows you to control only one very specific frequency at a time. It is composed of a series of slider faders, which are actually like volume controls. Each fader is assigned a frequency (e.g., 63Hz*, 500Hz, 8KHz), referred to as a "band," and hovers around a central point of reference. When you slide the fader up, the level of that frequency is raised; when you slide it down, it's lowered. In the middle, it's "flat." Obviously, the more bands you have, the more precisely you can manipulate your sound. They come in mono or stereo and, yes, they're available in digital, too.

Parametric EQs can determine the actual band*width,* so instead of boosting, say, just 10K, you can boost everything between 8.5K and 11K. Since this type of EQ is so versatile, it doesn't require a lot of bands. In fact I've recorded on $750,000 consoles that had only 4-band quasi-parametric EQs. You can find them a lot cheaper, though. I've also seen high-quality rack-mountable parametric EQ units, with *five* bands, for only about $350. Usually the bands are: lows, low-mids, high-mids, and highs. (The fifth band could be a "mid-mid.")

Other types of EQ include high-pass filters, low-pass filters, notch filters, even something called a "paragraphic" EQ. Most digital equalizers can create all kinds of EQ, often combining two or more kinds simultaneously. Check out all your options and see what you like (and need).

Compressor/Limiter. A compressor makes soft sounds louder and loud sounds softer. Virtually every major recording studio has some type of compressor/limiter. It can be a terrific enhancement to the sound of your bass, whether you're in the studio or on the gig. The effect narrows your range of volume, or "squashes" your sound. For example, if sometimes you're playing at 30dB (dB stands for decibels, the units for measuring volume) and sometimes you're playing at 100dB, you can use a compressor to shrink that audio range and keep everything between, say, 50dB and 80dB.

Here's how it works: When your volume level exceeds a certain level (called a "threshold"), the compressor steps in and lowers the output signal. The amount by which the signal is lowered is determined by the "compression ratio." A compression ratio of 5:1 (five-to-one) tells the compressor to raise the output by 1 dB for every 5 dB of input. If the quiet parts are too quiet, the overall level can be increased by turning up the "output" knob. The desired sound is attained by varying the compression ratio and the output level.

When the compression ratio is large enough, the compressor becomes a *limiter.* The job of a limiter is to prevent the signal from going too high, usually to avoid overloading amps or other equipment. Typical compression ratios for limiters are 10:1 and 20:1, though they could go much higher. Radio stations, for example, use "brick wall" limiting, which is boosting their signals as high as possible, without having to worry about broadcasting beyond their licensed power ratings.

Noise Gate. This device works on the same principle as a compressor. It has a threshold level, below which it won't "kick in." In other words, unless it receives a certain level of input (dBs), it will cut off any sounds in the signal flow. Noise gates are very practical for eliminating a hum or a high-pitched "hiss" that may be audible between musical phrases during quiet passages.

Other Effects. Most of the important effects have been covered, but here are a few more sounds you might want to investigate: Aural Exciter, Distortion, Harmonizer, Heavy Metal, Octave Divider, Overdrive, Pitch Changer, Phase Shifter, Vibrato, and Wah-Wah.

As I stated at the beginning, the intent of this appendix is to expose you to some of the equipment currently used by people in the music industry (bass players in particular), and to offer some insights into what you may (or may *not*) need. I hope now you'll be able to choose more carefully and buy more intelligently, without going too far, or getting talked into spending thousands of dollars on things you really don't need. Input from others is helpful, but when it comes to choosing *your* equipment, decide for yourself what it will take to do the trick. Who knows? You may even decide to buy only a Fender "Precision" and an Ampeg B-15. The novelty of it just might work!

---

* Hz is the abbreviation for Hertz, meaning cycles per second. K is short for KHz, or Kilohertz. One Kilohertz = 1,000 Hertz, or 1,000 cycles per second.

DISCOGRAPHY

Trying to play rock 'n' roll without knowing what it's supposed to sound like would be pointless. However, in light of the tremendous number of bands and the proliferation of records, tapes, CDs, and MP3s produced throughout the course of rock history, knowing what to listen to can be a daunting task, to say the least. With this discography, I've tried to make your job a whole lot easier by presenting you with a relatively brief list of carefully chosen recordings.

In the first five chapters of this book, I attempted to capture the essence of rock in each decade. This discography takes the same approach. For each decade, I've chosen several highlights of recorded music, typifying that period of rock 'n' roll. Wherever possible, I've also indicated the primary bassist(s). Keep in mind that this is *just a sampling* of the music of the artists and groups I felt were among the most important for each decade.

Since rock 'n' roll has always been an ongoing, forward-moving process, one cannot expect the history of rock to fit perfectly into nice, neat, ten-year "slots." Therefore, there is some overlap—a band in the "'80s" section, for instance, might contain recordings from the late seventies and/or the early nineties. What's more, certain acts, like Eric Clapton, Metallica and the Red Hot Chili Peppers, who have continued to have significant impact throughout their careers, may have entries in more than one decade.

At the end of each section is a listing called "*Also be sure to check out...,*" which provides a roster of other groups and artists that made important contributions to rock 'n' roll. Most of the recordings referenced here are readily available on CD and can also be found on iTunes, YouTube, Pandora, Spotfiy, etc. Listen and enjoy!

The '50s

Chuck Berry
> *St. Louis to Liverpool* (Chess)
> *Chuck Berry's Greatest Hits* (Chess)
> *Chuck Berry's Golden Decade* (Chess)

The Coasters
> *50 Coastin' Classics: Anthology* (Rhino)
> *The Very Best of the Coasters* (Rhino)

Bobby Darin
> *Splish Splash: The Best of Bobby Darin, Vol. 1* (Atco)
> *Mack the Knife: The Best of Bobby Darin, Vol. 2* (Atco)
> *As Long As I'm Singing: The Bobby Darin Collection* (Rhino, 4 discs)

Bo Diddley
> *Bo Diddley/Go Bo Diddley* (Chess)
> *The Chess Box* (Chess)

Fats Domino
> *They Call Me the Fat Man* (EMI, 4 discs)
> *Fats Domino: The Fat Man: 25 Classics* (EMI)

The Drifters
> *16 Greatest Hits* (Deluxe)
> *Greatest Hits* (Hollywood/Rounder)
> *Rockin' and Driftin': The Drifters Box Set* (Atlantic & Atco Remasters, 3 discs)

The Everly Brothers
> *Cadence Classics: Their 20 Greatest Hits* (Rhino)

Buddy Holly
> *The Buddy Holly Collection* (MCA, 2 discs)
> *Buddy Holly* (MCA)

Jerry Lee Lewis
> *Original Sun Greatest Hits* (Rhino)
> *All Killer, No Filler: The Anthology* (Rhino)
> *Jerry Lee's Greatest!* (Rhino)

Little Richard
> *The Georgia Peach* (Specialty)
> *The Specialty Sessions* (Specialty, 3 discs)
> *The Essential Little Richard* (Specialty)

The Platters
> *The Very Best of the Platters* (Mercury)

Elvis Presley
> *The Number One Hits* (RCA)
> *Worldwide 50 Gold Award Hits, Parts 1 & 2* (RCA)
> *Elvis—The King of Rock 'n' Roll—The Complete 50s Masters* (RCA)
> *The Complete Sun Sessions* (RCA)

Ritchie Valens
> *The Best of Ritchie Valens* (Del-Fi)
> *The Ritchie Valens Story* (Del-Fi)

Also be sure to check out ... The Big Bopper, Eddie Cochran, Danny & the Juniors, Bill Haley & the Comets, Carl Perkins, and Gene Vincent.

The '60s

The Animals (bassists: Bryan "Chas" Chandler, Danny McCulloch)
The Best of the Animals (MGM/Abkco)
The Best of Eric Burdon and the Animals, Vol. 2 (MGM)
The Greatest Hits of Eric Burdon and the Animals (MGM)

The Association (bassist: Brian Cole)
Greatest Hits (Warner Bros./Seven Arts)

The Beach Boys (primary bassists: Brian Wilson, Carol Kaye)
Surfin' Safari/Surfin' USA (Capitol)
Little Deuce Coupe/All Summer Long (Capitol)
Pet Sounds (Capitol)

The Beatles (bassist: Paul McCartney)
Please Please Me (Capitol)
Meet the Beatles (Capitol)
A Hard Day's Night (Capitol)
Help (Capitol)
Rubber Soul (Capitol)
Revolver (Capitol)
Sgt. Pepper's Lonely Hearts Club Band (Capitol)
The Beatles ("The White Album") (Capitol)
Abbey Road (Capitol)
Let it Be (Capitol)
The Beatles: 1962-1966 (Capitol)
The Beatles: 1967-1970 (Capitol)
1 (Capitol)
Also see: Paul McCartney (The '70s); Wings (The '70s)

Blood, Sweat & Tears (primary bassist: Jim Fielder)
Greatest Hits (Columbia)
The Best of Blood, Sweat & Tears: What Goes Up! (Columbia/Legacy, 2 discs)

Cream (bassist: Jack Bruce)
Fresh Cream (Polydor)
Disraeli Gears (Polydor)
Wheels of Fire (Polydor)
Goodbye (Polydor)
Strange Brew: The Very Best of Cream (Polydor)
Also see: Eric Clapton (The '70s , The '90s)

Creedence Clearwater Revival (bassist: Stu Cook)
Bayou Country (Fantasy)
Green River (Fantasy)
Cosmo's Factory (Fantasy)
Willie and the Poor Boys (Fantasy)
The Best of Creedence Clearwater Revival (Fantasy)

Donovan
Sunshine Superman (Epic)
Hurdy Gurdy Man (Epic)
Troubadour: The Definitive Collection 1964-1976 (Legacy)

The Doors
While this band, technically, had no bass player, the following bassists performed on many Doors recordings: Doug Lubahn, Jerry Scheff, Harvey Brooks, Kerry Magness, Larry Knechtel and Ray Neapolitan.
The Doors (Elektra)
Morrison Hotel (Elektra)
L.A. Woman (Elektra)
Best of the Doors (Elektra)

Bob Dylan
Bringing It All Back Home (Columbia)
Highway 61 Revisited (Columbia)
Blonde on Blonde (Columbia)
Bob Dylan's Greatest Hits (Columbia)

The Four Tops (primary bassist: James Jamerson)
Greatest Hits (Motown)
Anthology (Motown)

Tommy James & the Shondells (bassist: Mike Vale)
Hanky Panky/Mony Mony (Sequel)
The Very Best of Tommy James & the Shondells (Rhino)

Jefferson Airplane (bassist: Jack Casady)
Surrealistic Pillow (RCA)
The Worst of Jefferson Airplane (RCA)
2400 Fulton Street—An Anthology (RCA)
Jefferson Airplane Loves You (RCA, 3 discs)
The Essential Jefferson Airplane (RCA)

Jimi Hendrix (bassists: Noel Redding, Billy Cox)
Are You Experienced? (Reprise/MCA)
Axis: Bold as Love (Reprise/MCA)
Electric Ladyland (Reprise/MCA)
Band of Gypsies (Capitol)

The Kinks (primary bassist: Pete Quaife)
You Really Got Me (Reprise)
The Kinks Greatest Hits (Rhino)

Moody Blues (primary bassist: John Lodge)
Days of Future Passed (Deram/Polydor)
Seventh Sojourn (Threshold)
On the Threshold of a Dream (Deram/Polydor)
This Is the Moody Blues (Polydor)

Roy Orbison
The Legendary Roy Orbison (CBS Special Projects)
For the Lonely: A Roy Orbison Anthology (Rhino)
The All-Time Greatest Hits of Roy Orbison (Monument)

The Rolling Stones (bassist: Bill Wyman)
The Rolling Stones: England's Newest Hit Makers (Abkco)
Let it Bleed (Abkco)
The Rolling Stones, Now! (Abkco)
Big Hits (High Tide and Green Grass) (Abkco)
Hot Rocks: 1964-1971 (Abkco)
Also see: The '70s

Sly and the Family Stone (bassist: Larry Graham)
Stand! (Epic)
Greatest Hits (Epic)
Anthology (Epic)

The Supremes (primary bassist: James Jamerson)
Greatest Hits and Rare Classics (Motown)
Anthology (Motown)

The Temptations (primary bassist: James Jamerson)
Gettin' Ready (Motown)
Greatest Hits, Vol. 1 (Motown)
The Temptations Anthology (Motown)

Three Dog Night (bassists: Joe Schermie, Jack Ryland)
Harmony (Dunhill/MCA Special Products)
Celebrate: The Three Dog Night Story 1965-1975 (MCA)

The Who (bassist: John Entwistle)
My Generation (MCA)
The Who Sell Out (MCA)
Magic Bus (MCA)
Tommy (MCA)
Meaty, Beaty, Big and Bouncy (MCA)
Also see: The '70s

Stevie Wonder (primary bassist: James Jamerson)
Greatest Hits, Vol. 1 (Motown)

Greatest Hits, Vol. 2 (Motown)
Also see: The '70s

The Yardbirds (bassists: Paul Samwell-Smith, Chris Dreja)
Greatest Hits, Vol. 1: 1964-1966 (Rhino)
Vol. 2: Blues, Backtracks & Shapes of Things (Sony)

The Zombies (bassists: Paul Arnold, Chris White)
Time of the Zombies (Epic)
Greatest Hits (Digital Compact Classics)
Greatest Hits/Greatest Recordings (Transluxe)

Also be sure to check out … Booker T. & the MGs, James Brown, the Byrds, the Chiffons, the Dave Clark Five, Dion & the Belmonts, the Electric Prunes, the Fifth Dimension, the Four Seasons, Aretha Franklin, Freddie & the Dreamers, Marvin Gaye, Gerry & the Pacemakers, the Grass Roots, the Guess Who, Iron Butterfly, Janis Joplin, Gladys Knight & the Pips, Gary Lewis & the Playboys, the Lovin' Spoonful, the Mamas & the Papas, Manfred Mann, the Monkees, Procol Harum, the (Young) Rascals, Martha Reeves & the Vandellas, Paul Revere & the Raiders, Johnny Rivers, Smokey Robinson & the Miracles, Mitch Ryder & the Detroit Wheels, Simon & Garfunkel, Steppenwolf, Ten Years After, the Turtles, Vanilla Fudge, the Velvet Underground, Junior Walker & the All Stars, Mary Wells, and Jackie Wilson.

The '70s

AC/DC (bassist: Cliff Williams)
High Voltage (Epic)
Dirty Deeds Done Dirt Cheap (Epic)
Highway to Hell (Epic)
Also see: The '80s

Aerosmith (bassist: Tom Hamilton)
Aerosmith (Columbia)
Get Your Wings (Columbia)
Toys in the Attic (Columbia)
Rocks (Columbia)
Greatest Hits (Columbia)

Bachman-Turner Overdrive (primary bassist: C.F. "Fred" Turner)
Bachman-Turner Overdrive II (Mercury)
Bachman-Turner Overdrive: The Anthology (Mercury, 2 discs)

Bad Company (bassist: Boz Burrell)
Bad Company (Swan Song)
Straight Shooter (Swan Song)
Run with the Pack (Swan Song)
The Original Bad Company Anthology (Swan Song)

Black Sabbath (bassist: Geezer Butler)
Paranoid (Warner Bros.)
Master of Reality (Warner Bros.)
Vol. 4 (Warner Bros.)
Sabbath Bloody Sabbath (Warner Bros.)
We Sold Our Soul for Rock and Roll (Greatest Hits) (Warner Bros.)
Also see: The '80s, The '90s, The 2000s and beyond…

Boston (bassist: Fran Sheehan)
Boston (Epic)

Chicago (primary bassist: Peter Cetera)
Chicago Transit Authority (Columbia)
Chicago II (Columbia)
Chicago VI (Columbia)
Chicago VII (Columbia)
Chicago IX: Chicago's Greatest Hits (Columbia)

Eric Clapton (primary bassist: Carl Radle)
Layla and Other Assorted Love Songs (w/Derek & the Dominos) (Polydor)
Live at the Fillmore (w/Derek & the Dominos) (Polydor)
461 Ocean Boulevard (Polydor)
Slowhand (Polydor)
Timepieces: The Best of Eric Clapton (Polydor)
Crossroads (4 discs) (Polydor)
Also see: Cream (The '60s) and Eric Clapton (The '80s, The '90s)

Crosby, Stills, Nash (& Young) (primary bassists: Stephen Stills, Greg Reeves)
Crosby, Stills & Nash (Atlantic)
Déjà Vu (Atlantic)
So Far (Greatest Hits) (Atlantic)

Deep Purple (primary bassists: Roger Glover, Glenn Hughes)
Machine Head (Warner Bros.)
Made in Japan (Warner Bros.)
Who Do We Think We Are! (Warner Bros.)

Burn (Warner Bros.)
When We Rock, We Rock & When We Roll, We Roll
 (Greatest Hits) (Warner Bros.)

The Doobie Brothers (primary bassist: Tiran Porter)
Toulouse Street (Warner Bros.)
The Captain and Me (Warner Bros.)
Takin' It to the Streets (Warner Bros.)
Best of the Doobies (Warner Bros.)

**The Eagles (bassists: Randy Meisner,
 Timothy B. Schmit)**
Eagles (Asylum)
On the Border (Asylum)
Their Greatest Hits (1971-1975) (Asylum)
Hotel California (Asylum)
The Long Run (Asylum)
Also see: The '90s

**Electric Light Orchestra (primary bassist: Kelly
Groucutt)**
Face the Music (Jet)
A New World Record (Jet)
ELO's Greatest Hits (Jet)

Emerson, Lake & Palmer (bassist: Greg Lake)
Emerson, Lake & Palmer (Atlantic)
Tarkus (Atlantic)
Pictures at an Exhibition (Atlantic)
Trilogy (Cotillion)
Brain Salad Surgery (Atlantic)
*Welcome Back My Friends to the Show that
 Never Ends ... Ladies & Gentlemen* (Rhino)

Fleetwood Mac (bassist: John McVie)
Fleetwood Mac (Reprise)
Rumours (Warner Bros.)
Tusk (Warner Bros.)
Greatest Hits (Warner Bros.)

Peter Frampton (primary bassist: Stanley Sheldon)
Frampton Comes Alive (A&M)

J. Geils Band (bassist: Daniel Klein)
Full House (Atlantic)
Bloodshot (Atlantic)
The Best of the J. Geils Band (EMI)
Houseparty: The J. Geils Band Anthology
 (Atlantic & Atco Remasters/Rhino, 2 discs)

Grand Funk Railroad (primary bassist: Mel Schacher)
Grand Funk Railroad (Capitol Collectors Series)
Closer to Home (Capitol)
We're an American Band (Capitol)

Grateful Dead (bassist: Phil Lesh)
Workingman's Dead (Warner Bros.)
American Beauty (Warner Bros.)
The History of the Grateful Dead, Vol. 1 (Warner Bros.)

Heart (bassist: Steve Fossen)
Dreamboat Annie (Capitol)
Dog and Butterfly (Portrait)
Heart Greatest Hits/Live (Epic)

**Jethro Tull (primary bassists: Glenn Cornick,
 Jeffrey Hammond, John Glascock)**
Benefit (Chrysalis)
Aqualung (Chrysalis)
Living in the Past (Chrysalis)
Too Old to Rock 'N' Roll, Too Young to Die (Chrysalis)
M.U.: The Best of Jethro Tull (Chrysalis)

Elton John (primary bassist: Dee Murray)
Elton John (Uni)
Honky Chateau (Uni)
Goodbye Yellow Brick Road (Uni)
Greatest Hits, Vol. 1 (Uni)

Kansas (primary bassist: Dave Hope)
Leftoverture (Kirshner)
Point of Know Return (Kirshner)

Kiss (bassist: Gene Simmons)
Kiss (Casablanca)
Hotter Than Hell (Casablanca)
Dressed to Kill (Casablanca)
Alive! (Casablanca)
Destroyer (Casablanca)
Rock and Roll Over (Casablanca)

Led Zeppelin (bassist: John Paul Jones)
Led Zeppelin (Atlantic)
Led Zeppelin II (Atlantic)
Led Zeppelin III (Atlantic)
Led Zeppelin IV (Atlantic)
Houses of the Holy (Atlantic)
Physical Graffiti (Swan Song)
Led Zeppelin (boxed set) (Atlantic)
The Complete Studio Recordings (Atlantic)

**Lynyrd Skynyrd (bassists: Larry Junstrom,
 Leon Wilkeson, Ed King)**
Pronounced Leh'-Nerd Skin'-Nerd (MCA)
The Essential Lynyrd Skynyrd (MCA)
All Time Greatest Hits (Geffen)

Paul McCartney
McCartney (Capitol)
Ram (Capitol)
All the Best (Capitol)
Also see: The Beatles (The '60s); Wings (The '70s)

**Steve Miller (primary bassists: Lonnie Turner,
 Gerald Johnson)**
*Anthology: The Best of the Steve Miller Band
 (1968-1973)* (Capitol)
The Joker (Capitol)
Fly Like an Eagle (Capitol)
Book of Dreams (Capitol)
The Best of the Steve Miller Band 1974-1978 (Capitol)

Pink Floyd (bassist: Roger Waters)
Dark Side of the Moon (Harvest)
Wish You Were Here (Columbia)
The Wall (Columbia)

Queen (bassist: John Deacon)
A Night at the Opera (Elektra)
A Day at the Races (Elektra)
News of the World (Elektra)
Greatest Hits (Hollywood)

The Rolling Stones (bassist: Bill Wyman)
Sticky Fingers (Virgin)
Goats Head Soup (Virgin)
It's Only Rock 'n' Roll (Virgin)
Black and Blue (Virgin)
Some Girls (Polydor)
Also see: The '60s

Rush (bassist: Geddy Lee)
Rush (Mercury)
Fly by Night (Mercury)
Retrospective I: 1974-80 (Mercury)
Also see: The '80s, The '90s, The 2000s and beyond...

Santana (primary bassist: David Brown)
Santana (Columbia)
Abraxas (Columbia)
Santana III (Columbia)
Also see The '90s

Bob Seger (primary bassist: Chris Campbell)
Ramblin' Gamblin' Man (Capitol)
Smokin' O.P.'s (Capitol)
Beautiful Loser (Capitol)
Live Bullet (Capitol)
Night Moves (Capitol)

Bruce Springsteen (bassist: Garry Tallent)
Born to Run (Columbia)
Also see: The '80s

Steely Dan (primary bassists: Walter Becker, Chuck Rainey)
Can't Buy a Thrill (ABC)
Pretzel Logic (ABC)
Katy Lied (MCA)
The Royal Scam (MCA)
Aja (MCA)
A Decade of Steely Dan (MCA)

Rod Stewart (primary bassists: Ronnie Lane, Jay Davis, Carmine Rojas)
Gasoline Alley (Mercury)
Every Picture Tells a Story (Mercury)
Greatest Hits (Warner Bros.)
Storyteller: The Complete Anthology 1964-1990 (Warner Bros., 4 discs)

Supertramp (bassists: Frank Farrell, Dougie Thomson)
Crime of the Century (A&M)
Even in the Quietest Moments (A&M)
Breakfast in America (A&M)

Talas (bassist: Billy Sheehan)
Talas, featuring Billy Sheehan (Metal Blade)
Also see: The '90s

Talking Heads (bassist: Tina Weymouth)
More Songs About Buildings and Food (Sire)

Fear of Music (Sire)
Also see: The '80s

Toto (Bassist: David Hungate)
Toto (Sony)
Also see: The '80s

Robin Trower (bassist: Jim Dewar)
Bridge of Sighs (Chrysalis)

Van Halen (bassist: Michael Anthony)
Van Halen (Warner Bros.)
Van Halen II (Warner Bros.)
Also see: The '80s

The Who (bassist: John Entwistle)
Live at Leeds (MCA)
Who's Next (MCA)
Quadrophenia (MCA)
The Who by Numbers (MCA)
Who Are You (MCA)
30 Years of Maximum R&B (boxed set) (MCA)
Also see: The '60s

Wings (bassist: Paul McCartney)
Band on the Run (Capitol)
Venus & Mars (Capitol)
Wings over America (Capitol)
Wings at the Speed of Sound (Capitol)
Wings Greatest (Capitol)
All the Best (Capitol)
Also see: The Beatles (The '60s); Paul McCartney (The '70s)

Stevie Wonder (primary bassist: Nathan Watts)
Talking Book (Motown)
Innervisions (Motown)
Fulfillingness' First Finale (Motown)
Songs in the Key of Life (Motown, 2 discs)
Also see: The '60s

Yes (bassist: Chris Squire)
The Yes Album (Atlantic)
Fragile (Atlantic)
Close to the Edge (Atlantic)
Yessongs (Atlantic)
Going for the One (Atlantic)
Also see: The '80s

ZZ Top (bassist: Dusty Hill)
Tres Hombres (London/Warner Bros.)
Fandango! (London/Warner Bros.)
Tejas (London/Warner Bros.)
The Best of ZZ Top (London/Warner Bros.)
Deguello (Warner Bros.)
Eliminator (Warner Bros.)

Also be sure to check out ... the Allman Brothers Band, the Average White Band, Badfinger, Blue Öyster Cult, David Bowie, Jackson Browne, the Cars, Joe Cocker, Alice Cooper, Foghat, Foreigner, Genesis, Hall & Oates, Humble Pie, Jefferson Starship, King Crimson, the Steve Miller Band, Van Morrison, Ted Nugent, the Ramones, REO Speedwagon, Roxy Music, Todd Rundgren/Utopia, Paul Simon, Styx, Traffic, Uriah Heep, Edgar Winter, and Frank Zappa.

The '80s

AC/DC (primary bassist: Cliff Williams)
Back in Black (Epic)
For Those About to Rock, We Salute You (Epic)
Also see: The '70s

Black Sabbath (bassist: Geezer Butler)
Heaven and Hell (Warner Bros.)
Also see The '70s, The '90s, 2000s and beyond…

Bon Jovi (bassists: Alec John Such, Hugh McDonald)
Bon Jovi (Mercury)
7800° Fahrenheit (Mercury)
Slippery When Wet (Mercury)
New Jersey (Mercury)

Def Leppard (bassist: Rick Savage)
Pyromania (Mercury)
Hysteria (Mercury)
Vault 1980-1995 (Mercury)

Dire Straits (bassist: John Illsley)
Dire Straits (Warner Bros.)
Making Movies (Warner Bros.)
Brothers in Arms (Warner Bros.)

Duran Duran (bassist: John Taylor)
Duran Duran (Capitol)
Rio (Capitol)
Decade/Greatest Hits (Capitol)

Guns N' Roses (bassist: Duff McKagan)
Appetite for Destruction (Geffen)
Also see The '90s

INXS (bassist: Garry Gary Beers)
Listen Like Thieves (Atlantic)
Kick (Atlantic)
Greatest Hits (Atlantic)

Iron Maiden (bassist: Steve Harris)
Iron Maiden (EMI)
Killers (EMI)
The Number of the Beast (EMI)
Piece of Mind (EMI)
Powerslave (EMI)
Seventh Son of a Seventh Son (EMI)

Michael Jackson (primary bassist: Louis Johnson)
Off the Wall (Epic)
Thriller (Epic)
Bad (Epic)

Billy Joel (primary bassist: Doug Stegmeyer)
The Stranger (Columbia)
Greatest Hits Volume I & II (Columbia)

Journey (primary bassist: Ross Valory)
Escape (Columbia)
Greatest Hits (Columbia)
Time3 (Columbia, 3 discs)

Megadeth (bassist: David Ellefson)
Killing Is My Business...and Business Is Good! (Combat)

Peace Sells...But Who's Buying? (Capitol)
So Far, So Good...So What! (Capitol)
Also see: The '90s, The 2000s and beyond…

John (Cougar) Mellencamp
American Fool (Riva)
Uh-huh (Riva)
Scarecrow (Riva)
The Lonesome Jubilee (Mercury)

Metallica (bassists: Cliff Burton, Jason Newsted)
Kill 'Em All (Elektra)
Ride the Lightning (Elektra)
Master of Puppets (Elektra)
And Justice for All (Elektra)
Also see: The '90s

Mötley Crüe (bassist: Nikki Sixx)
Girls, Girls, Girls (Elektra)
Dr. Feelgood (Elektra)
Decade of Decadence—'81–'91 (Elektra)

Mr. Big (bassist: Billy Sheehan)
Mr. Big (Atlantic)
Also see: The '90s

Niacin (bassist: Billy Sheehan)
Niacin (Stretch)
High Bias (Stretch)

Ozzy Osbourne (primary bassist: Bob Daisley)
Blizzard of Ozz (Epic)
Diary of a Madman (Epic)
Bark at the Moon (Epic)

Tom Petty & the Heartbreakers (bassists: Ron Blair, Howie Epstein)
Damn the Torpedoes (Backstreet)
Hard Promises (Backstreet)
Full Moon Fever (MCA)
Greatest Hits (MCA)

The Police (bassist: Sting)
Regatta de Blanc (A&M)
Zenyatta Mondatta (A&M)
Ghost in the Machine (A&M)
Synchronicity (A&M)
Every Breath You Take: The Singles (A&M)
Message in a Box: The Complete Recordings (A&M, 4 discs)

The Pretenders (primary bassists: Pete Farndon, Malcolm Foster)
The Pretenders (Sire)
Learning to Crawl (Sire)
The Singles (Sire)

R.E.M. (bassist: Mike Mills)
Murmur (I.R.S./A&M)
Document (I.R.S.)
Green (Warner Bros.)
Add: Also see: The '90s

Rush (bassist: Geddy Lee)
Moving Pictures (Mercury)
Retrospective II: 1981–1987 (Mercury)
Also see: The '70s, the '90s, The 2000s and beyond…

Bruce Springsteen (primary bassist: Garry Tallent)
Darkness on the Edge of Town (Columbia)
The River (Columbia)
Born in the U.S.A. (Columbia)
Live, 1975-1985 (Columbia)
Tunnel of Love (Columbia)
Also see: The '70s

Sting (bassists: Sting, Darryl Jones)
Dream of the Blue Turtles (A&M)
Nothing Like the Sun (A&M)
Fields of Gold: The Best of Sting 1984-1994 (A&M)
Also see: The '90s

Talking Heads (bassist: Tina Weymouth)
Remain in Light (Sire)
Speaking in Tongues (Sire)
Stop Making Sense (Sire)
Popular Favorites 1976-1992: Send in the Vaseline (Sire)
Also see: The '70s

Toto (bassists: David Hungate, Michael Porcaro)
Toto (Columbia)
Toto IV (Columbia)
Past to Present 1977-1990 (Columbia)
Also see: The '80s

U2 (bassist: Adam Clayton)
The Joshua Tree (Island)
War (Island)
Rattle and Hum (Island)
Also see: The '90s

Van Halen (bassist: Michael Anthony)
Women and Children First (Warner Bros.)
Diver Down (Warner Bros.)
1984 (Warner Bros.)
5150 (Warner Bros.)
OU812 (Warner Bros.)
Best of Van Halen, Vol. 1 (Warner Bros.)
Also see: The '70s

Yes (bassist: Chris Squire)
90125 (Atco)
Big Generator (Atco)
Also see: The '70s

Also be sure to check out … Bryan Adams, Anthrax, Pat Benatar, Cinderella, Phil Collins, Elvis Costello, Dio, Dokken, Exodus, Peter Gabriel, Genesis, Sammy Hagar, Judas Priest, Cyndi Lauper, Huey Lewis & the News, Madonna, Yngwie Malmsteen, Motörhead, Poison, Queensrÿche, Quiet Riot, Ratt, the Scorpions, Skid Row, Slayer, Billy Squier, Tears for Fears, W.A.S.P., Whitesnake, and Steve Winwood.

The '90s

Alice in Chains (bassists: Mike Starr, Mike Inez)
Dirt (Columbia)
Jar of Flies (Columbia)

Black Sabbath (bassist: Geezer Butler)
Reunion (Epic)
Also see: The '70s, The 2000s and beyond…

Bush (bassist: Dave Parsons)
Sixteen Stone (Trauma)

Tracy Chapman (primary bassist: Andy Stoller)
Tracy Chapman (Elektra)
New Beginnings (Elektra)

Sheryl Crow
Tuesday Night Music Club (A&M)
Sheryl Crow (A&M)

Crowded House (bassist: Nick Seymour)
Woodface (Capitol)
Together Alone (Capitol)
Recurring Dream: The Very Best of Crowded House (Capitol)

Eric Clapton (bassist: Nathan East)
Unplugged (Warner Bros.)
Pilgrim (Reprise)
Also see: Cream (The '60s) and Eric Clapton (The '70s, The '80s)

Dream Theater (bassist: John Myung)
Images and Words (Atco)
Awake (EastWest)
Metropolis (Elektra)
Also see: The 2000s and beyond…

Eagles (bassist: Timothy B. Schmit)
Hell Freezes Over (Geffen)
Also see: The '70s

Goo Goo Dolls (bassist: Robby Takac)
Hold Me Up (Warner Bros.)
Superstar Car Wash (Warner Bros.)
A Boy Named Goo (Warner Bros.)

Green Day (bassist: Mike Dirnt)
Dookie (Reprise)
Insomniac (Reprise)

Guns N' Roses (bassist: Duff McKagan)
Use Your Illusion I (Geffen)
Use Your Illusion II (Geffen)
The Spaghetti Incident (Geffen)
Also see: The '80s

Hootie & the Blowfish (bassist: Dean Felber)
Cracked Rear View (Atlantic)
Fairweather Johnson (Atlantic)

Dave Matthews Band (bassist: Stefan Lessard)
Under the Table and Dreaming (RCA)

Crash (RCA)
Before These Crowded Streets (RCA)

Megadeth (bassist: David Ellefson)
Rust in Peace (Capitol)
Maximum Megadeth (Capitol)
Countdown to Extinction (Capitol)
Youthanasia (Capitol)
Hidden Treasures (Capitol)
Also see '80s, The 2000s and beyond…

Metallica (bassist: Jason Newsted)
Metallica (Elektra)
Load (Elektra)
Reload (SME)
Also see: The '80s, The 2000s and beyond…

Alanis Morissette
Jagged Little Pill (Maverick/Reprise)

Mr. Big (bassist: Billy Sheehan)
Lean Into It (Atlantic)
Bump Ahead (Atlantic)
Hey Man (Atlantic)
Also see: The '80s

Nirvana (bassist: Krist Novoselic)
Nevermind (DGC)
In Utero (DGC)
From the Muddy Banks of the Wishkah (Geffen/DGC)

Pantera (bassist: Rex Brown)
Cowboys From Hell (Atco)
Vulgar Display of Power (Rhino)
The Great Southern Trendkill (EastWest)
Far Beyond Driven (EastWest)

Pearl Jam (bassist: Jeff Ament)
Ten (Epic)
Vs. (Epic)
Vitalogy (Epic)
No Code (Epic)
Yield (Epic)
Rearviewmirror: Greatest Hits 1991-2003 (Epic)

Primus (bassist: Les Claypool)
Frizzle Fry (Caroline)
Sailing the Seas of Cheese (Interscope)
Pork Soda (Interscope)
Tales from the Punchbowl (Interscope)
Brown Album (Interscope)
Rhinoplasty (Interscope)
Antipop (Interscope)
Also see: The 2000s and beyond…

R.E.M. (bassist: Mike Mills)
Out of Time (Warner Bros.)
Automatic for the People (Warner Bros.)
Monster (Warner Bros.)
Also see: The '80s

Red Hot Chili Peppers (bassist: Flea)
What Hits!? (EMI)
Under the Covers: Essential Red Hot Chili Peppers (EMI)
Californication (Warner Bros.)
Also see: '80s, The 2000s and beyond…

Santana (bassist: Benny Rietveld)
Supernatural (Arista)
Also see: The '70s

Smashing Pumpkins (bassist: D'arcy Wretzky)
Siamese Dream (Virgin)
Melon Collie and the Infinite Sadness (Virgin)

Soundgarden (bassists: Hiro Yamamoto, Ben Shepherd)
Louder Than Love (A&M)
Badmotorfinger (A&M)
Superunknown (A&M)
Down on the Upside (A&M)

Sting
Ten Summoner's Tales (A&M)
Brand New Day (A&M)
Also see: The '80s

Stone Temple Pilots (bassist: Robert DeLeo)
Core (Atlantic)
Purple (Atlantic)
Tiny Music…Songs from the Vatican Gift Shop (Atlantic)

Talas (bassist: Billy Sheehan)
If We Only Knew Then What We Know Now (Metal Blade)
Also see: The '80s

U2 (bassist: Adam Clayton)
Achtung Baby (Island)
The Best of 1990-2000 (Island)
Also see: The 2000s and beyond…

Also be sure to check out … Beck, the Black Crowes, Blues Traveler, Collective Soul, Counting Crows, the Cranberries, Danzig, Gloria Estefan (Miami Sound Machine), Melissa Etheridge, the Gin Blossoms, Jane's Addiction, Korn, Lamb of God, Nine Inch Nails, Oasis, the Offspring, Papa Roach, Phish, Radiohead, Rage Against the Machine, Testament, the Verve Pipe, and the White Stripes.

The 2000s and beyond...

Avenged Sevenfold (bassist: Johnny Christ)
City of Evil (Warner Bros.)
Avenged Sevenfold (Warner Bros.)
Nightmare (Warner Bros.)

Black Sabbath (bassist: Geezer Butler)
13 (Universal Republic)
Also see: The '70s, The '80s, The '90s

Breaking Benjamin (bassist: Mark Klepaski)
Saturate (Hollywood)
We Are Not Alone (Hollywood)
Phobia (Hollywood)
Dear Agony (Hollywood)

Disturbed (bassists: Steve "Fuzz" Kmak, John Moyer)
The Sickness (Reprise)
Believe (Reprise)
Ten Thousand Fists (Reprise)
Indestructible (Reprise)
Asylum (Reprise)
The Lost Children (Reprise)

Dream Theater (bassist: John Myung)
Train of Thought (Elektra)
Octavarium (Atlantic)
A Dramatic Turn of Events (Roadrunner)
Dream Theater (Roadrunner)
Also see: The '90s

Fall Out Boy (bassist: Pete Wentz)
Take This to Your Grave (Sorepoint)
From Under the Cork Tree (Island)
Infinity On High (Island)
Folie à Deux (Island)

Five Finger Death Punch (bassist: Chris Kael)
The Way of the Fist (Firm Music)
War is the Answer (Spinefarm)
American Capitalist (Prospect Park)
*The Wrong Side of Heaven and the Righteous Side
of Hell* (Prospect Park)

Godsmack (bassist: Robbie Merrill)
Faceless (Universal)
IV (Universal)
The Oracle (Universal)

Green Day (Bassist: Mike Dirnt)
American Idiot (Reprise)
¡Uno! (Reprise)
¡Dos! (Reprise)
¡Tré! (Reprise)
Also see: The '90s

Halestorm (bassist: Josh Smith)
Halestorm (Atlantic)
The Strange Case of … (Atlantic)

The Killers (bassist: Mark Stoermer)
Hot Fuss (Island)
Sam's Town (Island)
Battle Born (Island)

Linkin Park (bassist: Dave "Phoenix" Farrell)
Hybrid Theory (Warner Bros.)
Meteora (Warner Bros.)
Minutes to Midnight (Warner Bros.)
A Thousand Suns (Warner Bros.)
Living Things (Warner Bros.)

Megadeth
TH1RT3EN (Roadrunner)
Super Collider (Tradecraft)

Also see: The '80s, The '90s

Mr. Big (bassist: Billy Sheehan)
Get Over It (2000)
Actual Size (WEA/Atlantic, 2001)
Back to Budokan (MSI: Frontiers, 2009)
What If… (Caroline, 2011)
Also see: The '80s, The '90s

Metallica (bassist: Robert Trujillo)
Some Kind of Monster (Universal)
Death Magnetic (Vertigo)
Also see: The '80s, The '90s

Niacin (bassist: Billy Sheehan)
Deep (Magna Carta)
Time Crunch (Magna Carta)
Organik (Magna Carta)
Krush (Prosthetic)
Also see: The '90s

Nickelback (bassist: Mike Kroeger)
All the Right Reasons (Roadrunner)
Dark Horse (Roadrunner)

Primus (bassist: Les Claypool)
Green Naugahyde (ATO)
Also see: The '90s

Red Hot Chili Peppers (bassist: Flea)
By the Way (Warner Bros.)
Greatest Hits (Warner Bros.)
Stadium Arcadium (Warner Bros.)
I'm With You (Warner Bros.)
Also see: The '90s

Rush (bassist: Geddy Lee)
Clockwork Angels (Roadrunner)
Also see: The '70s, The '80s

Skillet (bassist: John Cooper)
Comatose (Atlantic 2006)
Awake (Atlantic)
Alien Youth (Ardent)
Collide (Ardent)

Slipknot (bassist: Paul Gray)
Slipknot (Roadrunner)
Iowa (Roadrunner)
Vol. 3 (Subliminal Verses) (Roadrunner)
All Hope is Gone (Roadrunner)
Antennas to Hell (Roadrunner)

Stone Sour (bassists: Shawn Economaki, Rachel Bolan)
Come What(ever) May (Roadrunner)
House of Gold & Bones – Part 1 (Roadrunner)
House of Gold & Bones – Part 2 (Roadrunner)

Also be sure to check out … Adrenaline Mob, Arctic
Monkeys, Black Label Society, Blink 182, Bullet for My
Valentine, Cannibal Corpse, Coheed and Cambria, Coldplay,
Dethklok, Evanescence, Foo Fighters, Machine Head,
Maroon 5, Mudvayne, My Chemical Romance, Slayer,
Suicidal Tendencies, Three Days Grace, and White Zombie.

ACKNOWLEDGMENTS

Writing a book not only takes a lot of work, but also requires a lot of help. To all who offered their assistance in making this book a reality, I am truly grateful.

Thanks very much to guitarist *par excellence* **Jake Reichbart** and ace recording engineer/music consultant **Martin Liebman** (*yo, Bro!*). Well, guys, maybe it took a tiny bit longer in the studio than we had originally anticipated, but we documented history! Our combined talents and general camaraderie (along with similar tastes in meals, snacks, affinity for laughing in the face of "burnout," etc.) made recording the CD one of the most enjoyable and satisfying projects I've ever worked on. What do you guys think? Did that sound okay, Marty? How did that feel, Jake? Should we try it one more time? Let's hear it back…

Thanks also to those who took the time to proofread my manuscript and offer grammatical tweaks, perceptions regarding cultural significance and historical accuracy (not to mention pointing out blatant mistakes!). Thank you, **Mindy Liebman**, **Bob Palmateer**, **Tom Profit**, **Alisa Z** and **Randy Zdrojewski**. This book is much improved due to all of your input.

Thanks to all the incredible bass legends who studied my book, each thinking highly enough to give it his "seal of approval." Thank you, **Tim Bogert**, **David Ellefson**, **Tom Hamilton**, **Tony Levin**, **Marco Mendoza**, **John Moyer**, **Rudy Sarzo** and **Mike Watt**. Special thanks to **Billy Sheehan** for writing a heartfelt foreword for this new, revised edition. If there ever was a group of genuine bass royalty, it's all of you!

Thank you, **Randy Zdrojewski**, for your impeccable photographic skills, always getting the finished product just right; **Mike "Friedbaum" Friedman**, Detroit's wickedest drummer, for all the time you spent working through all those grooves and licks with me; **Dale Titus**, for (once again!) offering so many thoughts, suggestions and pointers; **Gary Graff**, nationally published award-winning music writer, for additional help and insights; **Belinda Lewoshko** of Magus Entertainment, **Lee Miller** of the Bass Place in Tempe, Arizona, and **Ron Bachman** of the Walk This Way Foundation.

Extra special thanks to my darling wife **Mindy** and to my great kids, **Josh**, **Rebecca**, **Emily** and **Adam**, for all your love and support. Thanks also for providing much-needed help with the music, drum programming and engineering, as well as setting me straight on what is – *and isn't* – cool (I'm still learning!). Thanks to my whole family. I love you all.

ABOUT THE AUTHOR

Jon Liebman is a world-renowned, bassist, composer, educator and entrepreneur. He has played electric and acoustic bass in every imaginable setting, from jazz gigs and club dates to full-scale concerts and internationally broadcast radio and TV shows. Jon has performed in many of the world's major concert venues, including New York's Madison Square Garden, LA's Shrine Auditorium and Tokyo's spectacular Suntory Hall (not to mention bull rings in Central America, amphitheaters in the Caribbean and all kinds of "off-beat" settings across the globe).

Throughout the course of a career that began over thirty years ago, Jon has performed and/or toured with a wide range of musical acts, including: Amy Grant, Cleo Laine, Buddy DeFranco, Ira Sullivan, Billy Eckstine, Eartha Kitt, The Drifters, The Platters, The Coasters, The Chiffons, The Ink Spots, The Fifth Dimension, Julio Iglesias, Jose Feliciano, Chita Rivera, Theodore Bikel, Ralphe Armstrong and countless others. Liebman has performed in the pit orchestras of many Broadway shows, including *Dreamgirls, Ain't Misbehavin', Phantom of the Opera, Les Miserables, Fiddler on the Roof, Oliver!, A Funny Thing Happened on the Way to the Forum, Golden Boy, Kiss of the Spider Woman, Annie* and many others. He has also supplied the bass tracks for major recording projects for clients which have included Ford, GM and the NBA, to name a few.

In addition to, **Rock Bass**, Jon has written five other books for Hal Leonard Corporation: **Funk Bass**, **Funk/Fusion Bass**, **Blues Bass**, **Bass Grooves: The Ultimate Collection** and **Bass Aerobics**. He is also the author of a book of transcriptions of the music of fellow bassist and good friend Stuart Hamm. A freelance writer and arranger, Jon's arrangements have been performed on *The Tonight Show, The Late Show* and other programs.

Jon Liebman has a Bachelor of Music degree in Jazz Studies & Contemporary Media from Wayne State University in Detroit and a Master of Music degree in Studio Music & Jazz from the University of Miami in Coral Gables, Florida. Jon has spent time in California, where he was active in the Los Angeles music scene as a performer and writer. He currently serves as Chairman/CEO of the Specs Howard School of Media Arts in Southfield, Michigan. Jon is also the founder of Liebman Media, LLC, anchored by the very popular www.ForBassPlayersOnly.com and www.JonLiebman.com websites. He lives with his wife Mindy and has four children.

ENDORSEMENTS

"Jon Liebman's wonderful book and accompanying CD, *Rock Bass*, is an essential tool for any bassist looking to expand their horizons as a player, or to reinforce all that they may already know into a more solid foundation. Sitting down and working your way through this book will most certainly bring new ideas and approaches to any bassist who takes the time. And it will be time well spent. Bass on!"
- **Billy Sheehan** (David Lee Roth, Steve Vai, Mr. Big, Niacin, the Winery Dogs)

"*Rock Bass* by Jon Liebman is a must-have for bassists of every generation and genre. The sections detailing the development of music as a reflection of the social and political events of each decade since the '50s alone is worth the price. The significant amount of information within the pages of this outstanding book and accompanying CD will help you define your unique role as a bass player. *I love this book!!!*"
- **Rudy Sarzo** (Ozzy Osbourne, Blue Öyster Cult, Quiet Riot, Dio)

Vocabulary in language is essential. The same holds true in music. The more musical 'words' you know, the better you'll be able to express yourself. You'll have more confidence when jamming with new people. You'll find yourself combining bits and pieces from different eras and styles into your own unique approach. Jon Liebman's *Rock Bass* will provide you with that vocabulary. It's completely packed with great riffs and runs from every planet in the pop music solar system. Whether you learn it from cover to cover or jump into each section as the need arises, you'll soon be 'speaking' the language. I wish I'd had this book when I was starting out!"
- **Tom Hamilton** (Aerosmith)

"Jon Liebman's *Rock Bass* book has a wonderful variety of bass lines to learn or play with, each in a pocket of its own. I like, too, how he's put them in all the keys, further helping players improve their chops."
- **Tony Levin** (King Crimson, Peter Gabriel)

"Jon has captured the essence of the evolution of rock bass styles as it was influenced by what was going on during each decade of rock & roll. If you weren't there, this book will give you an understanding of how it was and why we play what we do."
- **Tim Bogert** (Vanilla Fudge; Cactus; Beck, Bogert & Appice)

"I love the way *Rock Bass* recounts the historical events that gave rock & roll its spirit. The educational and user-friendly bass lines in this book should inspire players at all levels and help develop the ever-growing vocabulary of licks."
- **David Ellefson** (Megadeth)

"*Rock Bass* is a must-read, whether you are a beginner, intermediate or advanced pro bass player. It's full of important and comprehensive info!
- **Marco Mendoza** (Thin Lizzy, Whitesnake, Black Star Riders)

"Wanna try big time this stuff Jon Liebman's cooked for the rock side of bass guitar. Already digging his context, writing on the history side of things, which makes sense in lots of ways, especially for those just starting out who wanna get wet with more than just scales and transposed paint by numbers. Watt's view: Recommended!"
- **Mike Watt** (Iggy & the Stooges, the Minutemen)

"Not just a bass book, *Rock Bass* by Jon Liebman is a comprehensive rock music journey seen through the groove of the bass guitar. *Rock Bass* has the nuts, bolts and fundamental material to take anyone's playing to the next level. I am really impressed with this book!"
- **John Moyer** (Disturbed, Adrenaline Mob)

BASS NOTATION LEGEND

Bass music can be notated two different ways: on a *musical staff*, and in *tablature*.

THE MUSICAL STAFF shows pitches and rhythms and is divided by bar lines into measures. Pitches are named after the first seven letters of the alphabet.

TABLATURE graphically represents the bass fingerboard. Each horizontal line represents a string, and each number represents a fret.

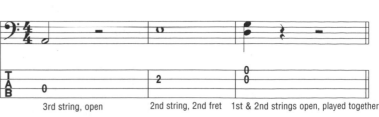

3rd string, open   2nd string, 2nd fret   1st & 2nd strings open, played together

HAMMER-ON: Strike the first (lower) note with one finger, then sound the higher note (on the same string) with another finger by fretting it without picking.

PULL-OFF: Place both fingers on the notes to be sounded. Strike the first and without picking, pull the finger off to sound the second (lower) note.

LEGATO SLIDE: Strike the first note and then slide the same fret-hand finger up or down to the second note. The second note is not struck.

SHIFT SLIDE: Same as legato slide, except the second note is struck.

TRILL: Very rapidly alternate between the notes indicated by continuously hammering on and pulling off.

TREMOLO PICKING: The note is picked as rapidly and continuously as possible.

VIBRATO: The string is vibrated by rapidly bending and releasing the note with the fretting hand.

SHAKE: Using one finger, rapidly alternate between two notes on one string by sliding either a half-step above or below.

NATURAL HARMONIC: Strike the note while the fret hand lightly touches the string directly over the fret indicated.

MUFFLED STRINGS: A percussive sound is produced by laying the fret hand across the string(s) without depressing them and striking them with the pick hand.

BEND: Strike the note and bend up the interval shown.

BEND AND RELEASE: Strike the note and bend up as indicated, then release back to the original note. Only the first note is struck.

RIGHT-HAND TAP: Hammer ("tap") the fret indicated with the "pick-hand" index or middle finger and pull off to the note fretted by the fret hand.

LEFT-HAND TAP: Hammer ("tap") the fret indicated with the "fret-hand" index or middle finger.

SLAP: Strike ("slap") string with right-hand thumb.

POP: Snap ("pop") string with right-hand index or middle finger.

ADDITIONAL MUSICAL DEFINITIONS

   (accent) • Accentuate note (play it louder)

   (accent) • Accentuate note with great intensity

   (staccato) • Play the note short

⊓ • Downstroke

∨ • Upstroke

D.S. al Coda • Go back to the sign (𝄋), then play until the measure marked "***To Coda***," then skip to the section labelled "***Coda***."

D.C. al Fine • Go back to the beginning of the song and play until the measure marked "***Fine***" (end).

Bass Fig. • Label used to recall a recurring pattern.

Fill • Label used to identify a brief pattern which is to be inserted into the arrangement.

tacet • Instrument is silent (drops out).

 • Repeat measures between signs.

 • When a repeated section has different endings, play the first ending only the first time and the second ending only the second time.

NOTE: Tablature numbers in parentheses mean:
1. The note is being sustained over a system (note in standard notation is tied), or
2. The note is sustained, but a new articulation (such as a hammer-on, pull-off, slide or vibrato begins, or
3. The note is a barely audible "ghost" note (note in standard notation is also in parentheses).